- THE -
WILD WORLD HANDBOOK

CREATURES

How Adventurers, Artists,
Scientists—And You—Can Protect
Earth's Animals

By Andrea Debbink

Illustrated by Asia Orlando

QUIRK BOOKS

PHILADELPHIA

OTHER BOOKS BY ANDREA DEBBINK

The Wild World Handbook: Habitats

Spark: A Guide to Ignite the Creativity Inside You

Think for Yourself: The Ultimate Guide to Critical Thinking in an Age of Information Overload

Library of Congress Cataloging-in-Publication Data

Names: Debbink, Andrea, author. | Orlando, Asia, illustrator.
Title: The wild world handbook : creatures: how adventurers, artists, scientists-and you-can protect
    earth's animals / by Andrea Debbink ; illustrated by Asia Orlando.
Description: Philadelphia : Quirk Books, [2021] | Series: The wild world handbook | Includes
    bibliographical references and index. | Summary: "A middle-grade guide to environmental
    stewardship and protecting diverse creatures"—Provided by publisher.
Identifiers: LCCN 2021012202 (print) | LCCN 2021012203 (ebook) | ISBN 9781683692683 (trade paperback) |
    ISBN 9781683692690 (epub)
Subjects: LCSH: Animals—Juvenile literature. | Wildlife conservation—Juvenile literature.
Classification: LCC QL49 .D394 2021 (print) | LCC QL49 (ebook) | DDC 590--dc23
LC record available at https://lccn.loc.gov/2021012202
LC ebook record available at https://lccn.loc.gov/2021012203

ISBN: 978-1-68369-268-3

Printed in China

Typeset in Argone, Hawkes, MVB Dovetail, and DTL Nobel

Designed by Elissa Flanigan

Illustrations by Asia Orlando and Elissa Flanigan

Production management by John J. McGurk

Quirk Books
215 Church Street
Philadelphia, PA 19106
quirkbooks.com

10 9 8 7 6 5 4 3 2 1

For my mom and dad, who
taught me to love wildlife

CONTENTS

INTRODUCTION
THE WORLD OUTSIDE

Humans share the planet with magnificent creatures. Some of earth's animals, however, are so commonplace it's easy to forget how incredible they are. The squirrels that people shoo from bird feeders are amazing acrobats who plant new trees by spreading seeds. The butterflies that pollinate gardens are resilient long-distance fliers who can cross a continent all alone. And the tree frogs that sing on summer nights can survive winter by freezing as solid as ice cubes and thawing out again in spring. Common or rare, beautiful to our eyes or not, all animals have parts to play in their habitats and in the world. When you stop to think about it, there's really no such thing as an ordinary animal.

In *The Wild World Handbook: Creatures* you'll learn about our world's wildlife. Some species will be familiar, and some creatures you might only ever see in nature documentaries or learn about in books. You'll read about people who have studied and protected wildlife such as a conservation biologist named Jamal who's saving endangered manatees, a herpetologist named Joan who taught people about misunderstood reptiles, and a writer named Beatrix who wrote illustrated books about animals and then used her earnings to protect nature. If you're inspired by their stories, this book also has ideas for how *you* can study and protect wildlife too.

When we take a closer look at our fellow animals, we discover how much we have in common. Like us, they live in communities, make friends, use tools, build homes, raise families, and communicate in complex ways. But this isn't all we share. We share habitats too. And humans have the ability to do great harm or great good to the environment we all depend on. Many animal species—from insects to polar bears—are in trouble because of climate change and other environmental threats like deforestation, overfishing, poaching, pollution, and disease. Sometimes the problems seem too big to solve. But as you may have read in *The Wild World Handbook: Habitats*, people just like you can solve intimidating problems when they use their creativity and skills to work with others and commit to long-term action. No matter what happens, it's important to keep protecting the habitats and creatures in our wild world. When we help animals and the places they live, we help ourselves too.

-CHAPTER 1-
INSECTS

Insects are the most common creatures on earth. Yet they often have a bad reputation. After all, an awful lot of insects bite, sting, and buzz in our faces. (Not to mention destroy the plants we grow for food.) But the bugs that cause harm are a small percentage of the world's insects. Most insect species do secret but important work that makes our lives possible. Without them, we couldn't exist. Insects pollinate plants, are food sources for other creatures, clean up waste in the environment, and create things that we use for food and medicine. Insects are useful—and they're also fascinating.

⫸⫸ INSECT FACTS ⫷⫷

1. Scientists have identified **MORE THAN 900,000** insect species—and more are being discovered every day!

2. Only one insect species lives on the planet's southernmost continent: a tiny fly with no wings called an **ANTARCTIC MIDGE**. It spends most of its life frozen in ice and covers its eggs in an antifreeze gel.

3. The very first creatures sent into space were **FRUIT FLIES**.

4. Spiders, ticks, mites, and scorpions may look like insects, but they're **ARACHNIDS**—a type of invertebrate animal that usually has eight legs.

5. At least one type of insect lives in families. Male and female **BESS BEETLES** not only take turns caring for their eggs, they also raise the baby beetles together after they hatch!

THE BUTTERFLY ARTIST
MARIA SIBYLLA MERIAN

APRIL 2, 1647–JANUARY 13, 1717

"In my youth, I spent time investigating insects."

—Maria Sibylla Merian

People said it was magic. They said the tiny creatures that appeared every summer were shapeshifters. What other explanation could there be? One day, nothing. The next day, the meadows were full of them, like delicate flowers that had fluttered right off their stems. Wings like soft petals. Fragile bodies as light as air. In the bright city gardens and the rolling farm fields, the creatures floated like fairies. In those days, people called them "summer birds." But they also used the name we know today: butterflies.

And what about the other mysterious creatures? The ones that crawled and crept, hurried and scurried and hid. They seemed to appear overnight, digging into the flour bin, spinning silvery webs in the corner of a window. Magic, people said. But bad magic. The kind you should stomp out with the heel of your shoe or sweep away with a broom.

An Unusual Hobby

In Frankfurt—in the country known today as Germany—lived a girl named Maria Sibylla Merian. When Maria saw insects, she wasn't afraid. She was curious about each one, especially butterflies and moths. Maria spent hours crouched amid the leaves watching caterpillars crawl and taking detailed notes. But she did this in secret. It was a strange hobby for a young girl in the 1600s—or anyone.

When Maria was growing up, people didn't know much about insects. And rather than study them, they invented stories and superstitions. The most common theory was called *spontaneous generation*. People thought insects—along with other animals such as frogs—were evil beings that were magically formed from dust or mud. But Maria didn't believe this.

Maria's stepfather was Jacob Marrel, a talented artist who was famous for his still-life paintings. In that time and place, there were unfair rules about what women were allowed to paint. But Jacob ignored these rules. He thought his stepdaughter had a gift and he encouraged Maria to paint the flowers and insects she loved. She studied art and nature, spending long hours outdoors. Since girls didn't attend school, she also studied natural history and Latin at home so she could read the scientific books of her day. (Back then, Latin was the universal language of science.) By the time Maria got married and had her first child, she was a successful watercolor artist who'd earned a reputation for her insect paintings.

The Mind of a Scientist

In those days, most nature artists observed dead specimens to create their art. Beetles and butterflies were killed and preserved like precious gems in special collections called *curiosity cabinets*. But Maria thought the best way to learn about insects was to study them in their natural habitats, to see how they lived. Maria took her art supplies into the fresh air, and in doing so, she made significant discoveries that other people missed.

During her observations, Maria witnessed a mysterious process scientists and scholars had begun to ponder, known as metamorphosis. *Metamorphosis* comes from a Greek word meaning "transformation." They noticed that some animals changed in dramatic ways. Maria had seen this for herself as she watched caterpillars become moths and butterflies. In 1679, when she was thirty-two years old, Maria published a book about metamorphosis called *The Wondrous Transformation of Caterpillars*, filled with illustrations of insects transforming from egg to caterpillar to pupa and finally to moths and butterflies. Eventually, Maria's work would help disprove the idea of spontaneous generation. Insects didn't magically appear, they came from eggs. And they weren't evil shapeshifters, they were intriguing animals.

Wealthy collectors bought Maria's art, and in turn, they shared their exquisite insect collections with her. It was in one collector's curiosity cabinet that

Maria first saw insects from Suriname, a small country on the northeast coast of South America, more than 4,700 miles away from her home in Amsterdam. The insects were unlike anything she had seen in Europe. One butterfly—brilliant blue and as large as her hand—was so beautiful it hardly seemed real. But Maria wasn't satisfied with admiring lifeless specimens. She wanted to study the living creatures in their own land.

In 1699, when she was fifty-two years old, Maria decided it was time to see Suriname for herself. In those days, there were few women explorers, and ocean voyages were dangerous and expensive. Maria paid for her expedition herself—selling more than 250 paintings—and invited along her daughter Dorothea. Maria spent two years exploring Suriname. She traveled by boat down winding rivers and on foot through the rainforest. When she was unable to find the insects she wanted, she paid local people to help her. And everywhere she went—in the lively city and in the lush jungle—she painted.

After Maria returned home, she published *The Metamorphosis of the Insects of Suriname*. The magnificent book contained sixty illustrations introducing European readers to the plant and insect life of South America. For the rest of her life, Maria lived in Amsterdam, where she owned a small shop and sold her art and specimens from her South American expedition.

Although Maria was a successful artist during her lifetime, her work as a scientist was mostly forgotten until the twentieth century. Today she is considered one of history's most important entomologists (scientists who study insects) and botanical illustrators, and her artwork is preserved in museums and libraries around the world. In addition, two species of spiders, a lizard, a toad, a plant, and a rare butterfly have been named in her honor.

THE SECRET OF THE
MONARCH BUTTERFLY

In Maria Sibylla Merian's lifetime, people wondered: "Where do butterflies come from?" Nearly three hundred years later, scientists tried to answer a similar question: "Where do butterflies *go*?" One of the most well-known butterfly species in North America is the **MONARCH BUTTERFLY**. It begins life as an egg, a black speck on the underside of a milkweed leaf. Then it hatches into a plump candy-striped caterpillar before finally turning into a butterfly. With orange wings as vivid as stained glass, monarchs flit through meadows all summer in Canada and the United States. Then one day, they suddenly disappear. Do they hibernate? Do they die? Until 1975, no one knew for sure.

In the 1920s, a Canadian teenager named Fred Urquhart often watched butterflies in the weeds along the railroad tracks near his home on the outskirts of Toronto. He wondered if monarchs migrated like birds. But where did they go? His question drove him to study biology and become a professor of zoology at the University of Toronto. Along the way he met and married Norah Roden Patterson, a fellow scientist who shared his curiosity. In the 1940s, they began their monarch research together.

The Urquharts' plan was to capture live butterflies and attach small paper tags to their wings. Each tag had an identification number and the university's mailing address. Fred and Norah hoped that when people found the butterflies along the migration route, they'd write to the university with information about the butterflies' locations.

Volunteers across the continent responded, and over the next several decades, the Urquharts and their research team discovered fascinating things

about monarchs, slowly mapping the butterflies' journeys through North America. Nearly forty years after Fred first wondered where the butterflies went, a pair of amateur naturalists—Kenneth Brugger and Cathy Aguado—found the answer. By the 1970s Fred thought the butterflies' winter destination was somewhere in Mexico. Kenneth and Cathy (now Catalina Trail) knew about the Urquharts' work and spent several years looking for the exact location.

In January 1975, while hiking in the Michoacán mountains, Kenneth and Cathy came upon a startling scene: millions of monarchs, draping across the trees like shimmering curtains. They had found the butterflies' destination at last! Nearly the entire monarch butterfly population of North America had traveled to just a few locations in the Michoacán mountains. One year later, the Urquharts visited one of the sites. Fred later said: "There, before my eyes, was the realization of a dream that had haunted me since I was sixteen."

In their decades of study, the Urquharts and their fellow researchers made several discoveries about monarchs:

- Unlike birds, monarchs migrate alone.

- Monarchs can fly more than 50 miles in a single day.

- It takes 3–4 generations of monarchs (each living for a month) to travel from Mexico to Canada. But it takes one generation to travel from Canada to Mexico—approximately every fourth generation lives for 9 months.

- Milkweed is the only food monarch caterpillars eat.

- Monarchs are in danger. Industrial farms along their migration route often use herbicides (chemicals that kill milkweed) and pesticides (chemicals that kill insects).

INVESTIGATE INSECTS

People have collected dead insects for hundreds of years—for scientific study and as a hobby. As you read in Maria Sibylla Merian's story, people often stored dead insect specimens in special display boxes called curiosity cabinets. (In fact, you can still see these collections in museums today.) But just as Maria discovered, it's more interesting—and better for the bugs—if you study living insects in their natural habitats. Explore your yard or a park using these tips:

INVESTIGATE PLANTS. Some of the best places to spot insects are on or near plants. That's where they get most of their food.

ZOOM IN. Most bugs are very small, so use a magnifying glass to get a closer look. (But keep your distance from insects that sting, such as wasps.)

CREATE A PHOTO COLLECTION. Take photos of what you find and create your own insect photo collection.

Bug Basics

Here are some common insects in the U.S. See if you can find these where you live—and remember to look, don't touch.

ANTS

Examples: carpenter ant, sugar ant, pavement ant, field ant.

BUTTERFLIES

Examples: monarch, Eastern tiger swallowtail, black swallowtail, cabbage white, spring azure.

MOTHS

Unlike butterflies, moths are mostly nocturnal! Examples: luna moth, sphinx moth, silk moth.

DRAGONFLIES

Examples: blue dasher, ebony jewelwing, pondhawk.

BEETLES

Examples: scarab, ladybug, firefly, ground beetle.

SPIDERS

Spiders are arachnids but they live in the same habitats as insects. Examples: jumping spider, American house spider, wolf spider.

THE LITTLE THINGS

The endangered animal species that make news headlines tend to be cute or cuddly or at least familiar. People often care less about **ENDANGERED INSECTS**. Unfortunately, many old-fashioned beliefs and fears about insects are still common—that they're bad, gross, destructive, or simply not important. But research has shown that insects are critical to the health of the planet. Here are some insects that people have protected.

Britain's Blue Butterflies

In 1979, a beautiful butterfly species, the large blue, became extinct in the United Kingdom, vanishing from meadows after its food source, a specific ant species, was wiped out. Once scientists discovered the cause of the butterflies' disappearance, they made plans to bring them back. In the mid-1980s, two ecologists transported blue butterfly eggs from Sweden to reintroduce them to the U.K. It worked! Thanks to their efforts and habitat conservation, the blue butterflies have made a comeback. Today the large blue butterfly's population in the U.K. is the highest it's been in more than eighty years.

Scotland's New Forest Burnet

Moths may be easier to overlook than their showy butterfly cousins, but both have a special place in nature. By 1990, a native moth species in Scotland called the New Forest burnet almost became extinct—there were only twenty left! Strangely enough, one thing that helped save the species was a fence. Sheep had overgrazed the areas where the moths lived. Once fences were built to keep out the sheep, the moths' population began to recover. Now there are about 2,000 New Forest burnet moths in Scotland.

New Zealand's Weta

In New Zealand, conservationists have worked hard to save the weta, a large insect that looks like a cricket. The largest variety is the Mahoenui giant weta, which is as big as a mouse—and behaves like one too. In fact, rodents are part of the reason weta are endangered in the first place. Rats and mice (first brought to New Zealand on ships hundreds of years ago) prey on weta and have pushed a few species close to extinction. But people are working to save the weta. Today weta are protected by the government, and there's a wildlife sanctuary dedicated to helping the weta's population recover. But what good is a weta? Part of the reason they're worth protecting is the answer to this question; we don't know yet. Like so many insects, weta haven't been studied much. But we do know they've been around since the age of the dinosaurs, and any species that's existed that long is worth learning about!

DIY

CREATE A COLLECTION

Early insect collectors filled cabinets with their specimens or pinned them to paper. Now we know that it's best to leave insects where we find them and admire them in the wild. But with a little creativity, you can still "collect" the ones you see.

Supplies

Card stock

Picture frame (without the glass)

Pencil

Colored pencils or markers

Scissors

Craft glue

Instructions

1. Cut a piece of card stock to fit inside the picture frame. Place the card stock inside the frame and fasten the back to hold it in place. (Use a small frame for a single "specimen" or a larger frame if you plan to build up a collection.)

2. Whenever you see an insect or take a photo of one, draw it on a piece of card stock. Use colored pencils or markers to color it in.

3. Use scissors to cut out the drawing. (If the insect has wings, fold the drawing lengthwise along the middle to give it a 3D effect.)

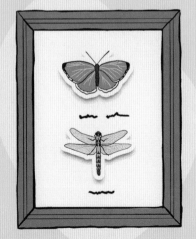

4. Use a dab of craft glue to attach the insect to the framed card stock. Write the name of the species underneath. Keep adding to your collection as you discover more insects! (Or use the insects you find to inspire your own imaginary versions.)

THE ENVIRONMENTAL WRITER
RACHEL CARSON

MAY 27, 1907–APRIL 14, 1964

"I could never again listen happily to a thrush song if I had not done all I could. And last night the thoughts of all the birds and other creatures and all the loveliness that is in nature came to me with such a surge of deep happiness that now I had done what I could."

—Rachel Carson

The waves were bigger than she expected. Sapphire blue and striped with foam, they heaved against the boat. This was Rachel's first time on the ocean, but it was her lifelong dream to hear the roar of the waves and to explore the sea. Rachel was a young marine biologist and she thought this research trip was the beginning of her career as a "poet of the sea," a title she'd invented for herself. But Rachel's life would take her ashore, and her world-changing work would focus on birds and flowers and some of the smallest creatures of all: insects.

Nature's Classroom

Rachel Carson was born in 1907 in a Pennsylvania farmhouse surrounded by countryside. Rachel spent her childhood writing stories inspired by Beatrix Potter and rambling through the fields and forests with her mother. Under the sunlit canopy of maples and oaks, her mother taught her to identify plants and animals. She told Rachel that all living things were connected and that even the smallest creature mattered.

Rachel never forgot her first lessons in nature. She also never forgot the awe she felt when she held one of her mother's prized possessions: a seashell that had somehow found its way to her family's fireplace mantel. When Rachel held the conch shell—its insides as smooth and pink as a rose petal—she imagined she could hear the voice of the ocean inside. Nature, it seemed, was full of wonders.

In 1925, Rachel enrolled in the Pennsylvania College for Women (now Chatham University) to study English. While in college, she took a biology class and became fascinated by science instead. She had loved nature all her life, but through biology she began to understand it in new ways. Rachel earned a degree in biology and became a researcher at a prestigious marine biology laboratory. Not only did she finally see the ocean, she began to learn its secrets.

But after Rachel earned a graduate degree in zoology, tragedy struck. The United States sunk into the Great Depression, and soon after that her father and sister died. Rachel became the only source of income for her mother and young nieces, and she set aside her dreams of ocean exploration and took an office job with the U.S. Department of Fisheries. She wrote scripts for radio broadcasts and scientific articles for magazines and newspapers. In 1937, a publishing house asked Rachel to turn one of her articles into a book. She spent the next few years writing a book about the ocean called *Under the Sea Wind*. Unfortunately, the book was published as the United States entered World War II, and although critics loved the book, it sold few copies.

"Miracle" Chemicals

After World War II ended in 1945, a new age of scientific discovery began. For centuries, insects such as mosquitoes, flies, and ants had destroyed crops and carried terrible diseases. But in the 1940s and '50s, scientists began creating new chemicals that could kill these insects, in hopes that the diseases would disappear and farms could produce more food. The new chemicals were called *pesticides*, and the most popular pesticide was known as DDT.

Most people thought DDT was a miracle chemical. It was colorless, tasteless, and odorless, and at first, it appeared to nearly eliminate diseases like malaria. In the United States, DDT was sprayed everywhere: planes dropped clouds of it on farm fields, trucks sprayed city streets until they were filled with a thick chemical fog, and people sprayed the insides of their homes (and even themselves) with it. The success of DDT encouraged the widespread use of even more pesticides.

Governments planned to exterminate certain insect species using pesticides—but they didn't consider the long-term effects. In the 1950s, the U.S. Department of Agriculture (USDA) tried to eradicate the fire ant, an invasive species that was ruining crops in the southern U.S., by spraying hundreds of thousands of acres with pesticide. This had shocking consequences; the pesticide killed not only fire ants, but birds, fish, and mammals too.

Rachel and other scientists had been suspicious of pesticides from the beginning. They thought the chemicals—particularly DDT—had entered the market too quickly with too little research. As a child, Rachel had understood that the natural world was interconnected. Now, as she studied the effects of pesticides, she saw that to harm one animal species meant to harm the whole habitat, whether you intended it or not.

Voice for the Environment

Since *Under the Sea Wind*, Rachel had written two more books and was a respected science writer. For four years, she researched DDT and other chemical pesticides. She worried about the damage they were causing to the food chain and how they could hurt people too. She also believed that chemical companies had purposely misinformed the public about their products' safety.

In her fourth book, *Silent Spring*, Rachel did what she did best— combine her scientific research with her ability to tell a story. And that story made a difference. Rachel began her book by inviting readers to imagine a silent world where birds and other creatures had been killed by pesticides. It was a sad scene, but it got people's attention. When *Silent Spring* was published in 1962, everyone was talking about it. Chemical companies protested it, the U.S. government questioned it, and people across the country read it. It was one of the first times in American history that a writer had communicated environmental concerns in a way the average person could understand. Rachel was invited to talk about her research on TV, and in 1963, she testified before Congress and asked the government to regulate the use of pesticides.

By the time Rachel died of cancer in 1964, *Silent Spring* had launched a movement. Her book led to the banning of DDT (though Rachel herself pushed only for its regulation) and to the creation of the Environmental Protection Agency, a U.S. government agency that oversees the country's health and environmental concerns. Perhaps most importantly, Rachel inspired people to look deep into the natural world and realize their part in it.

ADAM AND EVE

THE TREE LOBSTERS WHO SURPRISED SCIENCE

On Lord Howe Island in the Tasman Sea, between Australia and New Zealand, the stick insects grew so large that people called them "tree lobsters." The 8-inch-long nocturnal bugs skittered along tree trunks and through the island's undergrowth—until 1918, when a steamship made an emergency landing on the island. Rats escaped from the ship's hold and soon overran the island, eating every tree lobster they could find. And just like that, the Lord Howe Island stick insect became extinct.

Or so people thought. Rumors persisted, claiming there were tree lobsters living on a nearby sea stack. One night in 2001, four Australian scientists set out to see for themselves, traveling by boat to the sea stack and scaling its rocky sides. In the bright beams of their flashlights, they saw two tree lobsters! There were twenty-four in all. The species wasn't extinct, as people had believed, but it *was* in danger. This was the world's only known population of tree lobsters.

The scientists took four stick insects back to Australia to breed them and save the species. The first pair died, but the second pair was sent to the Melbourne Zoo. Scientists named them Adam and Eve. These two eventually produced thousands of offspring. Adam and Eve also helped researchers learn things about the species, such as what they eat and the fact that mating pairs form a bond (a rare behavior among insects). Scientists now hope to return captive-bred stick insects to Lord Howe Island—the descendants of two tree lobsters named Adam and Eve.

WAYS TO CARE

YOU: Be Kind to Wild Bees

You've probably seen a honeybee. But how about a blueberry bee or an orchard bee? There are 20,000 wild bee species in the world! Most are solitary, don't sting, and don't live in hives. Instead, they burrow into the ground, trees, or dead plant material. These bees are very efficient pollinators—even better than honeybees. And like their better-known cousins, wild bees are threatened by human activity. When the ground is covered with pavement or lawn, wild bees can't burrow into the ground to make their homes. You can help by leaving some uncovered areas of dirt in your yard or decaying leaves on the ground. Or build a "bee bath" to give bees water to drink and stay cool. Fill a saucer with a layer of stones. Place the saucer outdoors near plants and fill it halfway with water. Then wait for the bees to buzz by.

LOCAL: Grow Plants for Pollinators

Because insects are small, their work can go unnoticed. Yet their small jobs have big consequences—for nature and for us. Some insects—bees, butterflies, and moths—are known as *pollinators*. (Birds and bats are pollinators too.) These creatures depend on flower nectar for food. When a pollinator drinks nectar from a flower, it gets dusted with flower pollen and transfers the pollen from the male part of the plant (the anther) to the female part (the stigma). The plant can then create seeds that grow into more plants. Seventy-five percent of the crops humans eat depend on pollinators to reproduce. You can help pollinators by growing native plants (plants that naturally occur where you live)—and don't use chemical fertilizers or pesticides. Visit the National Wildlife Foundation's Native Plant Finder online to learn what plants to grow.

GLOBAL: Share Your Insect Knowledge

Insects are in trouble. One-third of the world's insect species are endangered because of habitat destruction, pesticides, and climate change. But we can help. One step is to spread the word about insects and the good work they do. Create a memorable slogan that teaches people why insects matter or describes a way people can help them. Use the slogan to create stickers, posters, T-shirts, or bracelets. Here are some environmental slogans from the past and present:

Give a Hoot—Don't Pollute!

Reduce. Reuse. Recycle.

Go Green!

Make Every Day Earth Day

CHAPTER 2
BIRDS

Birds bring color and life to our world. On every continent and in every habitat, birds fly, flock, and nest. Some, like the ostrich and the emu, are so large their wings can't lift them off the ground. Other birds are so small they'd be easy to mistake for moths. Everywhere birds live, they're a special part of the habitat. They pollinate plants, spread seeds, alert other animals to danger, control insect and rodent populations, and fill the air with their songs. They've shaped human life on land—and they've inspired us to take to the skies.

 BIRD FACTS

1. Birds aren't born knowing their calls and songs. They have to **LEARN** them—and practice!

2. The **BEE HUMMINGBIRD** is the world's smallest bird. It weighs less than a penny! One of the largest flying birds is the **WANDERING ALBATROSS**. Because of its mighty wingspan—up to 11 feet—it can spend hours in the air without flapping its wings even once.

3. A scientist who studies birds is called an **ORNITHOLOGIST**. But you don't have to be a scientist to study birds. Many discoveries have been made by amateur birders, people who watch birds as a hobby.

4. Birds have incredible **BRAINS**. Crows use tools to solve problems. Starlings can mimic complex sounds and songs. And chickadees can remember exactly where they've stashed food for up to 6 months.

5. Listening to **BIRDSONG** is good for you! Scientists have discovered that listening to the songs of some birds can make people more creative and relaxed.

THE BOLD BIRDER
FLORENCE MERRIAM BAILEY

AUGUST 8, 1863–SEPTEMBER 22, 1848

"In learning the Latin names, let us not forget the live bird."

—Florence Merriam Bailey

It was hard to ignore the feathers. The swooping ostrich plumes, the shimmering peacock feathers, and the most prized accessories of all: the gauzy feathers of the snowy egret. As Florence's college classmates paraded by, their hats bobbing with bird plumage, she had to hold her tongue. Florence believed feathers belonged on birds, not on people's heads. It would be easy for her to lecture her classmates about the way birds were ruthlessly hunted for their feathers. She had written magazine articles about it and argued for laws that would protect birds. But she had a different plan for changing her classmates' minds.

In 1886, Florence and a friend started a club: the Smith College Audubon Society for the Protection of Birds. (Later, small groups like this would join together to become the National Audubon Society, a bird conservation organization.) Florence didn't say a single word about feathered hats. Instead, she led her classmates on early-morning field trips to the nearby woods. She hoped that seeing wild birds would change their minds about wearing feathers.

Her plan worked. Florence's bird-watching trips became so popular she had to turn people away. By the end of that spring, many classmates had joined Florence in her activism. Together with many other groups across the country, their work led to the first national bird protection laws in the United States.

An Amateur Ornithologist

Florence Merriam Bailey was born in 1863 in Locust Grove, New York. In those days, wild birds were not widely admired and studied the way they are today. They weren't protected by the law either. People could hunt them however and wherever they wanted, and many hunters—called plume hunters—killed birds for their feathers. An ounce of feathers was worth its weight in gold! That's because in the late nineteenth century—especially in cities like New York and

London—fashionable women wore wispy feather tiaras, bonnets wreathed in pheasant wings, and even hats decorated with bird's bodies.

People didn't think it was possible to hunt birds out of existence. But that's exactly what they were doing. By the start of the twentieth century, more than five million North American birds were killed each year for their feathers, and some species—like the snowy egret—were near extinction. Eventually, 95 percent of Florida's shorebirds would be wiped out by plume hunting.

Changing people's minds about birds wasn't easy. The hat-making industry provided a lot of jobs and generated more than $17 million a year (that's more than $500 million today). And fashion wasn't the only business that depended on dead birds. Ornithologists paid hunters for dead specimens that they examined in labs or displayed in museums. Few people studied live animals in the wild.

Growing up in rural New York, Florence had learned that nature wasn't something to capture and collect. It was something to observe, explore, and protect. Her activism at Smith College was the beginning of her lifelong interest in bird conservation. Unlike other ornithologists, Florence didn't want to study dead birds in a lab. She thought there was a better way to learn about them.

Rather than pay a hunter for specimens, Florence headed to the woods with a notebook and small binoculars called opera glasses. (People used opera glasses to watch live theater, but Florence thought they came in handy for wildlife watching.) She dressed in drab clothing to camouflage herself in the forest's gray-green undergrowth. Then she sat quietly with her back against the strong trunk of a tree. Florence wrote down everything she noticed about birds: the markings on their feathers, their songs, how they raised their chicks, and what they ate.

Protecting Wild Birds

When Florence was in her early twenties, she became sick with a lung disease and traveled around Utah, Arizona, and California in search of a sunnier, drier climate to help her condition. Despite her illness, Florence wrote her first book in 1889 called *Birds through an Opera-Glass*. It was the first field guide to American birds, and it taught people how to study birds the way Florence did—quietly and patiently in their natural habitats.

That year, Florence married a naturalist named Vernon Bailey. They spent the next few decades camping throughout the U.S., studying birds and other wildlife. Florence wrote seven more books, including several field guides. She also taught ornithology classes for the National Audubon Society and continued to campaign for laws that protected birds. Today—because of a series of wildlife protection laws including the Migratory Bird Treaty Act—many bird species that were threatened during Florence's lifetime have recovered.

When Florence first followed birds into their natural habitats with her notebook and opera glasses, she didn't know she was starting something new. More than one hundred years later, bird-watching is one of the most popular nature activities in the United States. And thanks to people like Florence, generations of people have headed outdoors to learn about birds—with a curious mind and a pair of binoculars.

THE WORLD'S
MOST COLORFUL BIRDS

Birds come in every color of the rainbow. There are sunset-pink flamingos, iridescent green hummingbirds, and brilliant blue peacocks. There are also birds with muted colors like gray mourning doves and ink-black ravens. Each of these colors has a purpose. Usually it's to catch the eye of a potential mate (that's why male birds tend to be more colorful than female birds) or to provide camouflage.

A bird's color comes from **PIGMENTS** in its feathers, similar to the pigments in human skin, as well as from the way their feathers refract, or bend, light. (For example, bluebird feathers don't have blue pigment. Light makes the feathers appear blue to our eyes.)

Human eyes can see about one million colors—but birds can see even more than that! Birds see all the colors that humans see *plus* colors on the ultraviolet end of the spectrum. The following species are some of the world's most colorful birds. If they look colorful to us, imagine how they look to their fellow birds.

1. **MANDARIN DUCK** *Place of origin*: Japan, China, Russia

    The mandarin duck is native to Asia, but birds that have escaped captivity have created small flocks in Europe and North America.

2. **LADY GOULDIAN FINCH** *Place of origin*: Northern Australia

    This bird was named in honor of scientific illustrator Elizabeth Gould (see page 54). Before finch trapping was banned in Australia in 1981, thousands of Lady Gouldian finches were shipped around the world for pets.

3. LILAC-BREASTED ROLLER *Place of origin:* Southern and eastern Africa

The lilac-breasted roller feeds mainly on insects but will also eat snakes, rodents, and scorpions!

4. CRIMSON ROSELLA *Place of origin:* Southeastern Australia

This medium-sized parrot doesn't migrate. It spends the whole year in coastal and mountain forests.

5. INDIAN PEAFOWL *Place of origin:* India

Most people know this bird because of the bright blue male, which is known as the peacock. The female, the peahen, is dark green and brown.

6. PAINTED BUNTING *Place of origin:* Southern U.S. and Central America

The male painted bunting doesn't develop its bright colors until it's two years old.

7. RESPLENDENT QUETZAL *Place of origin:* Central America

The brilliant green resplendent quetzal has tail feathers that are longer than its body.

8. GOLDEN PHEASANT *Place of origin:* Western China

This beautiful bird is a clumsy flyer, so it prefers to run along the ground.

9. AMERICAN GOLDFINCH *Place of origin:* North America

Male American goldfinches grow bright yellow feathers in the spring and shed them in the fall.

10. FLAMINGO *Place of origin:* U.S., Central America, Africa, Asia, Europe

The flamingo's famous pink feathers come from the algae it eats. Healthy, well-fed flamingoes have more brightly colored feathers.

ALEX

THE PARROT WHO HAD AN INCREDIBLE BRAIN

One summer day in 1977, Dr. Irene Pepperberg bought a parrot at a Chicago pet store and named him Alex. He was a one-year-old bird with smoke-gray feathers and curious round eyes. Parrots had been popular pets for centuries because of their companionship and ability to mimic human language. But Dr. Pepperberg didn't bring home the African grey parrot simply to have a pet. She was an animal psychologist who studied the way birds think and behave. Over the next few decades, Alex formed a strong bond with Dr. Pepperberg. But he also taught her—and the world—about the amazing bird brain.

Bird brain used to be an insult because people had long believed that birds weren't smart. In the past, scientists assumed that birds were a little like preprogrammed robots. They thought birds acted only on instinct and were unable to think in complex ways. Birds like Alex have proven them wrong. Dr. Pepperberg studied Alex for more than thirty years. She discovered that African grey parrots think in ways that are similar to dolphins and apes, two animal families that are known for their intelligence. Alex had a bold personality and a sharp mind. He learned to say more than one hundred words, identify shapes and colors, respond to questions, do simple math, and express emotion. "Clearly, animals know more than we think," Dr. Pepperberg once wrote, "and think a great deal more than we know."

LEARN TO SPOT BIRDS

Depending on where you live, you probably see or hear birds when you go outside—whether it's a pigeon in a park or a sparrow at a bird feeder. Florence Merriam Bailey was one of the first nature writers to teach people how to watch and identify birds (see page 40). Now, more than 100 years later, bird-watching (or "birding") is a popular activity around the world. And it's more than a fun hobby: amateur bird-watchers often collect important scientific data.

You can be a bird-watcher too. Go on a bird-watching walk or watch the birds outside your window. Gather the following clues, then use a bird field guide or an app such as Audubon Bird Guide to help you identify the birds you see.

COLOR

What color is the bird? Keep in mind that the male and female of the same species can look different from each other. Also, some bird species are more brightly colored in the summer, when they're trying to attract a mate.

SIZE

A bird's size is a clue to its identity, but don't worry about trying to measure one. Instead, picture an American robin, one of the most common North American birds. A robin is a medium-sized songbird that's about 10 inches long from beak to tail. When you see a bird you don't recognize, compare it to a robin. Is the bird larger or smaller?

SHAPE

The shape of a bird's body, head, tail feathers, and beak can all help identify the species.

LOCATION

Think about where you are in the world. Many bird species live only in certain geographic areas. Then notice the habitat where you see the bird. Is it in the woods, in an open field, near water?

BEHAVIOR AND HABITS

What is the bird doing? Is it searching for food in the grass or does it eat from a bird feeder? Does it gather in groups or is it alone? These details matter because not all birds eat, nest, fly, or socialize in the same way.

SOUNDS

A bird's song or call is another helpful clue. Compare what you hear to bird sounds on apps like Merlin Bird ID. But keep in mind that some bird species can mimic other birds' calls. That's why it helps if you can hear *and* see the bird you're trying to identify.

NORTH AMERICA'S
BALD EAGLES

High in the branches of an oak tree is one of the largest bird nests in the world. It's more than 5 feet across and weighs close to 2,000 pounds. A pair of **BALD EAGLES** returns to it each spring to raise chicks. Nests like this—and the powerful birds who make them—are common throughout North America.

Throughout history, the eagle has been a sacred animal to many Indigenous cultures and has long been a symbol of courage and strength. The bald eagle has been the national bird of the United States since 1782. But without the work of conservationists, America's bald eagles would only be symbols today, not real birds that still fly in our skies. That's because in the 1960s, bald eagles almost became extinct.

The bald eagle, whose name comes from its recognizable white head, is the only eagle that's native to North America. Their population first fell in the late 1800s because of unrestricted hunting and destruction of their habitat. Some people hunted bald eagles for trophies, and others killed them because they mistakenly believed the birds preyed on livestock. (Eagles prefer to eat fish and smaller birds.) Despite the passage of the Bald Eagle Protection Act in 1940, which made it illegal to hunt them, these birds continued to face threats in the 1940s and '50s. Pesticides like DDT poisoned many animals across the United States, and because bald eagles ate poisoned fish and mammals, they produced eggs that weren't healthy enough to hatch. By 1963, there were just 487 nesting pairs left in the lower 48 states. If people didn't take action, America's national bird would become extinct.

Thanks to the efforts of activists like Rachel Carson (see page 28), the U.S. government banned DDT in 1972. A year later, Congress passed the Endangered Species Act and included bald eagles in its list of protected creatures. Eagle nesting sites became protected places and conservationists reintroduced eagles to areas where they had disappeared. Decades later, there are more than 9,000 nesting pairs in the lower 48 states. It's a comeback story worth celebrating—and learning from.

Bald eagles aren't the only birds that have been saved through conservation efforts. Here are some others:

- **WHOOPING CRANES:** In 1941, there were 21 whooping cranes left in the wild; now there are now more than 600.

- **BROWN PELICANS:** By the 1970s, there were no longer any brown pelicans in Louisiana and very few along the Texas coast. Today these states have 12,000 nesting pairs.

- **KIRTLAND'S WARBLERS:** Forty years ago, there were only 167 nesting pairs of this small songbird. Now there are more than 2,000.

CROCHET A BIRD'S NEST

Nests are safe places for birds to raise their young—and they're works of art. Birds have the ability to gather materials like mud, twigs, moss—even spider silk!—and use them to build complex structures. And just as there are many different types of birds, there are many different types of nests. The American robin builds a new nest every year with twigs and mud. Orioles weave pouches that hang from branches. Loons build nests on islands or floating logs. And plovers make nests by scraping a shallow hole in gravel, sand, or shells.

In spring and summer, it's not unusual to see baby birds that have left the safety of their nests. If the birds are on the ground and have feathers, it's likely they're *fledglings*, young birds that are learning to fly. It's normal for these birds to be left alone by their parents throughout the day. But sometimes, baby birds are injured or orphaned. When people find birds like this, they often take them to wildlife rehabilitators or the local humane society. You can help these birds by using your creativity.

Wildlife rehabilitation centers often use homemade yarn "nests" to keep young birds warm and secure. They depend on volunteers to make these nests. All you need is a crochet hook and cotton or acrylic yarn. There are many video tutorials online that will show you how to make the nests. Before you get started, make sure there's a local wildlife rehabilitator or humane society that's accepting nest donations. You can find a licensed wildlife rehabilitator near you by visiting the Humane Society's website: humanesociety.org.

THE FORGOTTEN ORNITHOLOGIST
ELIZABETH GOULD

JULY 18, 1804–AUGUST 15, 1841

The ornithologist John Gould's illustrated books were some of the most beautiful in the world. They had page after page of extraordinary birds like finches from the Galápagos Islands and vibrant Australian hummingbirds. In the mid-1800s, before the invention of color photography, books like John's introduced nature's wonders to people who would never see them in real life.

John was honored throughout the world for his expert knowledge and remarkable books. But in the pages of his famous books was a secret. Many of the illustrations were created by an anonymous scientific illustrator who never received formal credit: his wife, Elizabeth.

Bringing Birds to Life

Elizabeth Gould was born in England in 1804. Little is known about her early life other than that her father served in the British military and that she had ten siblings. It's likely that Elizabeth was educated because in that time and place, girls of her social class would have learned a limited set of skills that included foreign languages, music, drawing, and watercolor painting.

Elizabeth married John Gould in 1829 when they were both twenty-four years old. John was a young ornithologist who worked at a museum and owned a taxidermy shop, where he preserved animal specimens for collectors. In England at that time, people were fascinated by nature, and ornithology—the study of birds—was a new specialized science. As the United Kingdom colonized other countries, animal specimens were collected and sent to British museums, libraries, universities, and wealthy collectors. One of John's jobs was to preserve these specimens. Soon after they were married, he asked Elizabeth to create illustrations of his taxidermy work that they could sell in the shop. Already a talented amateur artist, Elizabeth rose to the challenge.

In 1830, John collected bird specimens from India and decided to create his first illustrated book. Back then, scientific illustrators and writers usually based their work on dead specimens, not live animals. The book was an incredible undertaking and he couldn't do it alone. Publishers were using a new—and painstaking—printing process called *lithography* that allowed them to make vibrant color copies of original art. This process required artists to trace their drawings onto stone and hand-color the final print with watercolor paint. John's book took five years to make and required a staff of several people. Elizabeth drew and painted the illustrations for the book. It was the largest artistic project she'd ever done, yet she was not given credit as the book's illustrator.

The book, *A Century of Birds from the Himalaya Mountains*, was so successful that John decided to immediately begin work on another book. This time he focused on the birds of Europe. Elizabeth and John spent months traveling around the continent studying birds and creating illustrations. For the first time Elizabeth had the chance to observe and paint birds in their natural habitats, and it showed in the liveliness of her illustrations.

John's second book, *Birds of Europe*, was completed in 1837, and once again Elizabeth was not named among the book's artists. It became a pattern. Later that year, John needed Elizabeth's help with another project. A naturalist named Charles Darwin had returned to England with bird specimens from the Galápagos Islands, in the Pacific Ocean west of Ecuador. John was hired to study the birds, and he identified them as a new species. He asked Elizabeth to illustrate the birds for Darwin. When Darwin later published a book about his scientific findings, it included many detailed bird illustrations. No credit was given to the artist, Elizabeth Gould.

In 1838, the Goulds went on a three-year expedition to Australia. Elizabeth was reluctant to go because it meant leaving their three youngest children behind with their grandmother. But John needed Elizabeth's help on his next book. This one featured the birds of Australia, and he had realized how important it was to study and illustrate these animals in their natural habitats. Once again, John researched and wrote the text and Elizabeth (along with an assistant named Edward Lear) created most of the illustrations. They returned to England in 1840. Sadly, Elizabeth died of a sudden illness the following year, leaving behind John, their many children, and the unfinished book.

A Secret Legacy

John Gould lived for another forty years. Throughout his life, he made many contributions to ornithology, publishing nearly a dozen books and more than 300 scientific papers. He was nicknamed "the Bird Man," and because of his groundbreaking research in Australia, he's also been called "the father of Australian ornithology."

But the illustrations that launched John's publishing career and earned him his artistic reputation were made by Elizabeth. She was a skilled and knowledgeable scientific illustrator at a time when most women were excluded from scientific study. Her role in John's work was largely overlooked—or unknown—until the middle of the twentieth century. Yet her invisible work moved the study of ornithology forward. It's difficult to say what Elizabeth thought about her lack of recognition. The few letters she wrote and her private diary don't mention her art or her feelings on the topic. But today her memory lives on in a bird that John named in her honor—the colorful Lady Gouldian finch—and in the beautiful and educational art she created.

STEWARDSHIP

WAYS TO CARE

YOU: Protect Birds from Pets

One of the most common threats to songbirds is a cat or dog looking for a plaything—or a meal. If your family has a pet, make sure someone supervises it when it's outside so that it doesn't harm birds or other wildlife. There are also special collars for cats and dogs that use bells or bright colors to alert birds to the pet's presence.

LOCAL: Make Windows Bird-Safe

One of the biggest dangers to birds might seem harmless: windows. In the U.S. and Canada, more than one billion birds die each year because they collide with windows. (Birds see trees and sky reflected in the glass and think they can fly through.) But people are developing solutions to this problem, such as creating bird-safe glass. To the human eye, this special type of glass looks clear, like a normal window. But to a bird's eye, it appears to have a pattern and breaks up reflections. Some buildings that have switched to this new glass have seen a 90 percent reduction in bird collisions! But you don't have to install new windows to help birds at home. One easy way to make windows safer is decorate them with vinyl clings or reflective tape that's specifically designed to reduce bird collisions (available at hardware and home improvement stores). These products make windows visible to birds, so they won't try to fly into the glass.

GLOBAL: Be a Birder

Scientists who study birds depend on volunteers to help collect information about bird populations and behavior. Become a citizen scientist and join one of the following projects led by the Cornell Lab of Ornithology or the Audubon Society. For each of these projects, volunteers record their observations and submit them through a website or app.

Project FeederWatch: Keep track of the birds that come to bird feeders during winter and spring. (feederwatch.org)

NestWatch: Count the bird nests where you live and report on what you find. (nestwatch.org)

The Great Backyard Bird Count: For four days each February, volunteers all over the world join together to count the birds where they live. (birdcount.org)

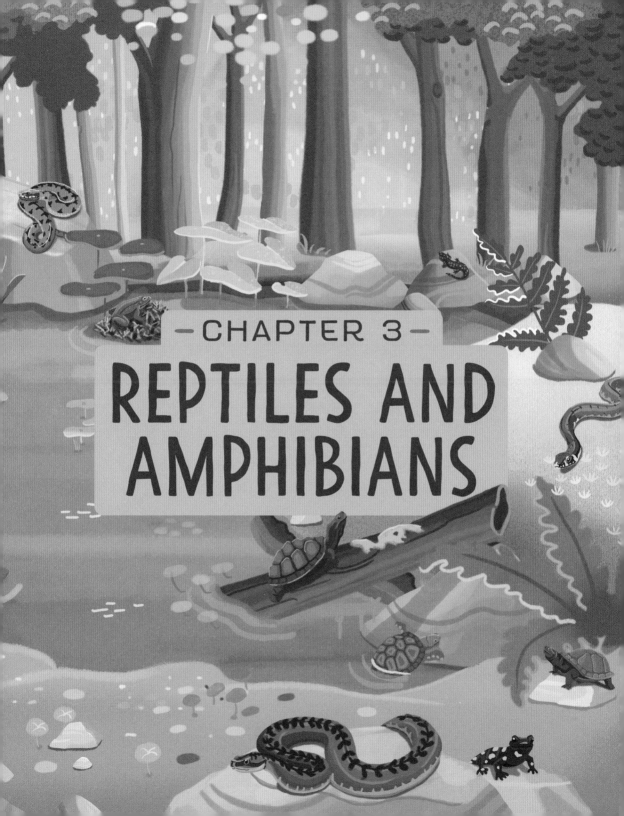

-CHAPTER 3-
REPTILES AND AMPHIBIANS

Dinosaurs no longer walk the earth, but there are still creatures with skin like armor, claws like daggers, and very sharp teeth: reptiles. The name *reptile* comes from an Old Latin word that means "to creep or crawl." They live in almost every habitat in the world. But they're not alone. There's another group of animals that creeps and crawls: amphibians. Their name comes from the Greek word *amphibious*, which means "living a double life." Most amphibians begin their lives in water but undergo metamorphosis and are able to live on land too. Reptiles and amphibians have a lot to teach us about the past *and* the present.

REPTILE AND AMPHIBIAN FACTS

1. Reptiles include creatures like crocodiles, snakes, lizards, turtles, and tortoises. There are **MORE THAN 10,000** reptile species.

2. There are **MORE THAN 8,000** amphibian species, including many species of frogs, toads, newts, salamanders, and caecilians (wormlike creatures that live underground in tropical regions).

3. Reptiles and amphibians are **ECTOTHERMIC**, sometimes called "cold-blooded." This means they depend on external sources, like sun and shade, to regulate their body temperature.

4. A cold reptile is a slow reptile—and vulnerable to predators. But, amazingly, there are reptiles that live north of the Arctic Circle. One species is the European adder. In the far north, this common snake hibernates for **8–9 MONTHS**!

5. Amphibians are very **SENSITIVE** to environmental changes so scientists study them in order to know if an ecosystem is healthy.

THE REPTILE PROTECTOR
JOAN BEAUCHAMP PROCTER

AUGUST 5, 1897–SEPTEMBER 20, 1931

"To the minds of many people, the word dragon suggests a purely mythical beast. . . . And yet almost all fictitious dragons are based on living reptiles."

—Joan Beauchamp Procter

In Joan Beauchamp Procter's London neighborhood in the early 1900s, it was not unusual to have a pet. People walked poodles in the park, kept chattering birds in cages, and owned cats that slept in sunny windows. But only Joan had a pet crocodile.

Joan received the crocodile when she was 16 years old. It wasn't her first reptile. When Joan was very young, she played with pet lizards and snakes instead of dolls. She never knew what a lizard would do next. It might sit quietly for hours in the sun or catch a fly with its tongue as quick as a wink. Or it may dart away and disappear. Joan loved all reptiles—all creatures that crawled and slithered along the ground with sandpaper skin or smooth scales. Joan's crocodile was named Ramases, and he went wherever Joan did. That is, until he grew too large and had to start a new life at the zoo. Years later, Joan would find her place at the zoo, too.

An Unlikely Herpetologist

Joan didn't know anyone who liked reptiles as much as she did. The only person who came close was a famous zoologist named Dr. George Boulenger, who was the keeper of reptiles and fishes at the Natural History Museum in London. When Joan was a teenager, she wrote to Dr. Boulenger about reptiles and sometimes visited him at the museum with her pets in tow. He was impressed with her inquisitive mind and how much she knew about animals.

Joan dreamed of attending Cambridge University, but she was unable to leave her London home because of her health. She had a lifelong intestinal illness, and when it flared up, she'd become sick and weak. Even though Joan couldn't attend college, she didn't stop learning. In 1916, Dr. Boulenger invited Joan to become his assistant at the museum, and she jumped at the chance. Two years later, with Dr. Boulenger's guidance, she published her first scientific paper—about pit vipers—with the Zoological Society of London. She was just 19 years old. In 1920, Dr. Boulenger retired and Joan was hired to replace him, becoming the first woman curator of reptiles at the museum.

Saving Dragons

As Joan worked at the museum, she also helped at the nearby London Zoo. By then, Joan had a reputation as both a respected herpetologist (a scientist who studies reptiles and amphibians) and an artist. She was skilled at technical drawing, making 3D models, and designing imaginative exhibits. In 1923, Joan was hired to be the zoo's curator of reptiles and amphibians. As the first woman reptile curator, Joan became a celebrity to zoo visitors, and she was admired for her fearless ability to handle dangerous animals like pythons and crocodiles.

At the zoo, Joan started the project that would become her biggest legacy: a new reptile house. When she began working at the zoo, its reptile habitats were in poor shape; the cold-blooded reptiles and amphibians weren't getting the sunlight they needed, and their dirty enclosures were making them sick. Joan knew what to do. Working alongside an architect, she combined her scientific knowledge with her artistic skill to design a state-of-the-art reptile habitat. When the reptile house was completed in 1927, visitors and scientists from around the world marveled at its groundbreaking design. It had freshwater pools, heated rocks, modern lighting, tropical plants, a veterinary clinic, and windows with a new kind of glass that allowed UV rays to pass through. (Reptiles need UV light to be healthy.)

Not long after the reptile house opened, the zoo received an unusual delivery all the way from Indonesia: a pair of Komodo dragons! British scientists knew very little about these giant reptiles (they had only learned of their existence in 1912), and Joan had only ever seen their pictures in books. But now, she had to figure out how to take care of the 7-foot lizards. The dragons were in rough shape from their long sea voyage from Asia. "When the dragons arrived, they were ill and miserable," Joan said, "so we gave them warm baths, drinks, and medical attention."

Komodo dragons had a fearsome reputation, and the first scientists who had studied them were afraid of the lizards. Not Joan. She thought they were beautiful and regal. She named the dragons Sumba and Sumbawa after two Indonesian islands. Under her care, the pair grew healthy and strong. In fact, all the zoo's reptiles became healthier, more active, and more content in Joan's reptile house.

The pair of Komodo dragons became Joan's companions as she worked at the zoo. They'd gently take food from her hand and even let her pet their heads and tails. Sometimes, Joan would walk Sumbawa around the zoo's grounds, "steering" the lizard by her tail! And curious visitors, even young children, were allowed to touch the dragons and see them up close. The lizards were powerful animals that could be fierce, but Joan showed people that they were interesting creatures, not ruthless monsters.

When she was in her late twenties, Joan became sick with cancer. But even as she grew weaker, she continued her work at the zoo. She would make her usual rounds using a wheelchair, with Sumbawa walking at her side like a faithful dog. Joan died in 1931, but her work lives on at the London Zoo and in our understanding of the reptiles she studied and loved.

THE LONG LIVES OF REPTILES

Some reptiles alive today are more than 100 years old, including a tortoise, a crocodile, and a rare lizard-like reptile called a tuatara. In the animal kingdom, long lives are not common. Some insects live for only a few weeks or months. Some birds and mammals live for a few years. Even the average human lifespan is around 80 years. But the world's oldest living reptile is 109 years older than that!

The world's oldest living reptile also holds the record for the world's oldest land animal. He's a **SEYCHELLES GIANT TORTOISE** named Jonathan (*opposite, bottom*), and biologists believe that he was born on an island in the Seychelles, in the Indian Ocean, in 1832. (That means he's 189 years old!) He was brought to his current home—St. Helena, an island in the South Atlantic—in 1882 as a gift for the governor of the island. Today Jonathan is a much-loved local celebrity and still lives on the grounds of the governor's residence with three other giant tortoises: Emma, David, and Fred.

It's not uncommon for giant tortoises to live for 100 years, but Jonathan's story is amazing because his age is nearly twice that. Yet he's not the only long-lived reptile in the world. Crocodiles are another reptile species known for their long lives. The oldest known living crocodile is named Henry, and he's 120 years old. He's a **NILE CROCODILE** (*opposite, middle*) that was first captured by a hunter in 1903. (He supposedly had a reputation for attacking people.) Since 1985, he has lived at a zoological park in South Africa in the company of other crocs.

In New Zealand, there's another reptile named Henry that's estimated to be 120 years old. He is a **TUATARA** (*opposite, top*), an animal that is found only in New Zealand. *Tuatara* is a Māori word meaning "peaks on the back." Henry has been living at a museum with other tuataras since 1970. Incredibly, he became a parent for the first time when he was 111 years old.

Why do reptiles like these live so long? No one knows for sure, but scientists have some ideas. First, none of these species has any real predators (although rats eat tuatara eggs and hatchlings). Second, they grow very slowly compared to other animals and take a long time to reach adulthood. Scientists think that their low body temperatures and slow metabolisms cause them to age more slowly, because they burn less energy over the course of their lifetimes than other animals. Imagine the stories they could tell!

LONESOME GEORGE

THE TORTOISE WHO WAS THE LAST OF HIS KIND

Giants once roamed Ecuador's Galápagos Islands—tortoises that grew to be 4 feet long and could weigh 700 pounds. They were so plentiful that the islands were named after them; *galápago* is the Old Spanish word for "tortoise." The Galápagos are one of two places in the world where giant tortoises live. Over the centuries, sailors captured them for food and brought animals such as rats and goats to the islands that destroyed tortoise habitat and ate their eggs. By the late 1960s, one species—the Pinta Island tortoise—appeared to be extinct. Then in 1971, a scientist spotted a lone tortoise wandering the island's volcanic landscape.

The tortoise became known as "Lonesome George." Researchers brought him to a tortoise research center on a neighboring island and hoped to find a female Pinta Island tortoise so they could save the species. But as the years passed, it sadly became clear that George was the very last animal of his species.

For decades, George lived alongside other giant tortoises in an outdoor habitat at the research center. When he died in 2012, the Pinta Island tortoise became extinct. In his life and his death, George became a symbol for wildlife conservation, reminding people what can happen when animals and their habitats are not protected.

LISTEN TO FROG SONGS

The music begins in early spring. It starts with a chorus of rusty squeaks. Then a rippling refrain that sounds like a phone's ringtone. A thumping bass keeps time, and one high note soars above the rest. It's the frog and toad chorus, and it might sound like a bunch of noise—unless you know what to listen for.

Frogs and toads are their loudest in spring and early summer, when males can be heard trying to attract female mates with their calls. The animals can be difficult to spot, but you don't need to see them in order to figure out which species they are. Instead, you can identify frogs and toads by listening.

In spring or early summer, find a place where you can hear frogs or toads in the early evening. This might be in your neighborhood or a park. Depending on where you live, you might be able to hear their calls through an open window without even leaving the house. Listen quietly and count how many different calls you hear. What do they sound like? A squeak, or sleigh bells, or a snapping rubber band? Once you can pick out one particular call, the easiest way to identify it is to match it to a recording on a website or app like FrogID. With practice, you'll be able to identify frog calls without help. Here are some common North American frogs and toads. Look up their calls to see if any of them sound familiar.

AMERICAN TOAD: A very common toad that can live in varied habitats from forests to grasslands.

Sounds like: A vibrating whistle.

BULLFROG: The biggest frog in North America, the bullfrog can weigh up to two pounds!

Sounds like: A cello playing one note.

NORTHERN LEOPARD FROG: Leopard frogs get their name from their pattern of dark spots.

Sounds like: A small motor.

SPRING PEEPER: This common species of chorus frog is one of the first to start calling each spring.

Sounds like: Sleigh bells.

TREE FROGS: There are about 30 species of tree frogs in the U.S. Two common species are the gray tree frog and the Pacific tree frog.

Sounds like: A ringing phone (gray tree frog) or a squeaky spring (Pacific tree frog).

WOOD FROG: Woods frogs have the amazing ability to freeze in cold weather and thaw when the temperature rises!

Sounds like: A clucking chicken.

WOODHOUSE'S TOAD: This toad species has a large population and lives throughout North America.

Sounds like: A high-pitched snore.

ALLIGATORS
OF THE AMERICAN SOUTH

The **AMERICAN ALLIGATOR** has always made its home in the sunny fresh-water habitats of the southern United States. (Once upon a time they lived as far north as New Jersey!) They hunt for fish and crustaceans in Louisiana bayous, sun themselves in Florida wetlands, and float in Mississippi backwaters. With impressively sharp teeth and strong jaws that can snap a turtle shell in half, the American alligator is one of the most powerful predators around. But not long ago, North America's largest reptile was in danger of being hunted to extinction. Like so many animals, until people made up their minds to save it, it might've disappeared altogether.

In the 1950s and '60s, there was a high demand for American alligator meat and products like boots and belts that were made from the reptile's tough skin. Their population dropped so low the federal government outlawed alligator hunting in 1967. A few years later, alligators received even more legal protection when the Endangered Species Act was created.

But poachers continued to threaten alligators across the southern U.S., and the reptiles disappeared from some of the places they once lived. A combination of efforts eventually turned the tide. The government started captive breeding programs to restore the population, passed laws that protected alligator habitats, and allowed for alligator farms. (Though the latter was not popular with environmentalists, the farms helped protect wild alligators from poachers.) People also stopped buying as many alligator products and began to better understand the alligator's role in freshwater habitats. By 1987, the alligator population had recovered so much that they were removed from the endangered species list.

Today there are more than one million alligators in the United States. But the country's human population has increased too, and people often move into (or accidentally create) ideal alligator habitats. Within its range, an alligator will live nearly anywhere there is water and food, which includes places like golf courses and swimming beaches. With increasing interactions between alligators and humans, it can be easy to see them as nuisance animals.

But these reptiles are incredibly important to the ecosystem. As apex predators (meaning they're at the top of the food chain), they help control the populations of rodents and other animals that might destroy plant life. Alligators also dig burrows called *gator holes* that become water reservoirs for other animals during dry seasons. Without them, these habitats wouldn't be the same. When people decided to save alligators, they ended up saving so much more.

MAKE A TOAD ABODE

Toads are common creatures, but they are very good at hiding and are most active at night. If you have a yard or garden, they're a good animal to have around because they help control insect populations. These secretive creatures are most comfortable when they have places to hide such as a fallen log, dirt burrow, or leaf pile. If you want to help toads where you live, make a house where a toad can take shelter.

Supplies

Terra-cotta flowerpot

Nontoxic craft paint
  (assorted colors)

Paintbrushes

Trowel or small shovel

Saucer (optional)

Instructions

1. Cover your workspace and clothing before you begin. Then use craft paint and paintbrushes to decorate the outside of the flowerpot. You only need to paint half of it. Let it dry for about 24 hours.

2. Choose the location for your toad house. It's best to place the house in a shady spot near plants where toads can burrow into loose soil.

3. Use the trowel to dig a shallow hole. Turn the flowerpot on its side and bury the unpainted half. Make sure the flowerpot is secure in the soil and doesn't move around. (You wouldn't want to accidentally make a toad trap.)

4. Place some dead leaves or dried grass inside the toad house. You can also place a saucer of water nearby. (The saucer from the bottom of the flowerpot will work well.) Then it's time to wait for the toads. They're usually looking for new homes in spring and summer.

THE CROCODILE CONSERVATIONIST
STEVE IRWIN

FEBRUARY 22, 1962–SEPTEMBER 4, 2006

"I've been put on this planet to protect wildlife and wilderness areas,
which in essence is gonna help humanity."

—Steve Irwin

The Irwin family's new home was crowded. Not just with people, but with animals. A dozen baby kangaroos snuggled into homemade pouches. Koalas climbed the curtains. Snakes coiled in cages along the walls. Sometimes without warning, a sugar glider would leap through the air and land on eight-year-old Steve's back as he walked through the living room. But he didn't mind. Steve loved sharing his home with animals.

Steve's parents, Bob and Lyn, had moved their family to a small plot of land on Australia's Sunshine Coast. Their dream was to open a wildlife park where they would rehabilitate injured or orphaned animals and teach people about misunderstood creatures like reptiles. Opened in 1970, the Beerwah Reptile Park had small beginnings. At first, the Irwin family lived in a camper on two acres of land and charged visitors just 50 cents to see their exhibits.

Steve grew up caring for the family's wildlife and helping his dad capture reptiles for research or to relocate them. He had caught his first snake—a venomous brown snake—when he was just four years old. The unexpected incident scared Bob, but it also made him realize there was something special about his son. Steve Irwin not only loved animals; he had a gift for understanding them.

The Crocodile Hunter

Like his dad, Steve was fascinated by reptiles. Australia is home to 800 reptile species, including snakes, lizards, and crocodiles. Creatures like these were often seen as pests. If crocodiles made their homes in populated areas, they were often killed. Poachers also hunted them for their skin and meat. In the 1970s, saltwater crocodiles were nearly wiped out in Australia. Conservationists like the Irwins worked to save them.

Crocodiles were Steve's favorite animals, and he was an expert at understanding and handling these dangerous reptiles. When he was a young man in the 1980s, he volunteered with the government's crocodile relocation program. In his work with the program, Steve saved more than 100 crocodiles by relocating them to wildlife parks or less populated parts of the country.

When he wasn't saving crocs in the wild, Steve worked at his family's wildlife park, and in 1991, he became manager of the park. (It was later renamed Australia Zoo.) That same year, an American woman named Terri Raines visited the park and met Steve during a crocodile demonstration. Terri ran a wildlife rehabilitation center in the United States and shared Steve's passion for wildlife conservation. A few months after Terri and Steve met, they got married. Their first big adventure together was a crocodile rescue mission in northern Queensland, where they relocated a 15-foot crocodile. They brought along a film crew to record the experience, and it became the very first episode of a new kind of wildlife documentary: *The Crocodile Hunter.* Eventually, Steve and Terri would film more than 300 episodes of wildlife documentaries, many of them featuring Steve's beloved crocodiles.

Steve thought the best way to get people to care about animals was to share his enthusiasm rather than lecture his audiences. And as a TV host, that's exactly what he did. More than 500 million viewers watched Steve and Terri travel the world, explore wildlife habitats, and rescue crocodiles. Steve became known for his fearlessness. He'd catch venomous snakes by the tail, swim with sharks, and leap out of the way just as a crocodile snapped its jaws—sometimes using his trademark phrase, "Crikey!" Eventually Steve and Terri had two children, a daughter named Bindi and a son named Robert. Just like Steve, they grew up at a wildlife park and shared their parents' dedication to animals and conservation.

A Conservation Legacy

Despite his worldwide fame, Steve's dreams were always bigger than a TV series or running a popular wildlife park. He wanted to protect wildlife and habitats everywhere and invite others to join him. In 2002, he and Terri started a nonprofit organization—known today as Wildlife Warriors Worldwide—that raises funds for conservation projects and operates a world-class wildlife hospital at Australia Zoo. (The hospital rehabilitates and releases more than 7,000 Australian animals each year.) The Irwins also purchased large areas of land to create wildlife refuges.

In 2006, Steve died unexpectedly in an accident while filming a documentary near the Great Barrier Reef. People around the world felt as if they had lost a hero and a friend. Since then, Steve's family and friends have continued his mission and his wildlife work. Terri continues to lead the work at Australia Zoo, and Bindi and Robert have followed in their parents' footsteps as wildlife conservationists. They know that Steve would be proud. "Steve knew that what he was trying to do was much bigger than himself. It's bigger than us," Terri says. "It's trying to protect the planet and make positive change."

STEWARDSHIP

WAYS TO CARE

YOU: Let Wildlife Be Wild

Catching frogs, toads, snakes, salamanders, and turtles—and keeping them as pets—sounds like fun. After all, they're interesting creatures to watch and investigate. But the truth is wild animals belong in the wild. An animal like a frog or turtle will be much happier and healthier in its natural habitat than in a bucket or aquarium. So if you find one of these animals outside, take time to watch it, but leave it outdoors. It's better for the animal and for the ecosystem.

LOCAL: Study Frogs

Frogs and other amphibians are very sensitive to their environment. When frogs are unhealthy or absent from an ecosystem, it often means that the ecosystem is unhealthy. That's why it's important for scientists to study frogs—and you can help! FrogWatch USA is a national citizen science program in which volunteers keep track of the frogs they hear twice a week throughout spring and summer. The data that volunteers collect is used by scientists. Ask a parent or guardian to join you, or ask your teacher. It could be a fun project for your whole class. Find more information at www.aza.org/frogwatch.

GLOBAL: Protect Reptile and Amphibian Habitats

Amphibians are becoming extinct faster than any other animal. (More than half of the world's amphibian species are nearing extinction.) One of the biggest causes is a dangerous pathogen called chytrid fungus that infects (and kills) amphibians. But habitat loss and climate change play a role in extinction too. One of the simplest ways to help amphibians (and reptiles) on a global scale is for people to protect local amphibian and reptile populations. Here are a few ideas.

Organize a trash clean-up in parks that have wetlands or waterways.

Ask your family not to use harmful chemicals or pesticides on the lawn or in gardens.

Leave natural ground cover (like dead wood and decaying leaves) whenever possible.

Keep pets away from wild amphibians and reptiles.

Never release a reptile or amphibian from a pet store into the wild. Nonnative species can hurt local populations and can introduce diseases like chytrid fungus.

-CHAPTER 4-
LAND ANIMALS

No matter where you go in the world, whether you camp in a forest, drive through a desert, bike through a city, or swim in a sea, you'll meet a mammal. (You'll also see one if you look in the mirror—humans are mammals, too.) There are more than 6,000 mammal species and most of them live nearly all of their lives on land. With complex brains and the ability to maintain a constant body temperature, mammals are some of the most adaptable animals on earth. Land-dwelling mammals can live in leafy treetops, dark underground caverns, and everywhere in between.

⇶ LAND ANIMAL FACTS ⇷

1. Mammals are **ENDOTHERMIC**, which sometimes is called being "warm-blooded." This means their bodies can maintain their own temperature. Mammals also have backbones and fur or hair, and they feed their young with milk.

2. Another name for land animal is **TERRESTRIAL ANIMAL**. *Terrestrial* comes from the Latin word *terra* which means "earth." To be a terrestrial animal means "to be of the earth."

3. About **40 TO 50** new mammals are discovered each year. Sometimes this is because scientists will document a new species in the wild (like the lesula, a monkey in the Democratic Republic of Congo), but often it's because they reclassify and rename known species as they learn more about them.

4. All terrestrial mammals move across land in different ways. Depending on the species and their habitat, they can **WALK**, **RUN**, **JUMP**, **CLIMB**, **SWIM**, and **TUNNEL** through the ground.

5. The largest mammal on land is the **AFRICAN ELEPHANT**. It can be up to 13 feet tall and weigh up to 7 tons. That's almost as much as 3 minivans. The smallest land mammal is the **BUMBLEBEE BAT**. As you might guess, it's about the size of a bumblebee!

THE STORYTELLING NATURALIST
BEATRIX POTTER

JULY 28, 1866–DECEMBER 22, 1943

"I do not remember a time when I did not try to invent pictures and make for myself a fairyland amongst the wild flowers, the animals, fungi, mosses, woods and stream, all the thousand objects of the countryside."

—Beatrix Potter

Beatrix crumpled the letter and tossed it aside. Her friend's son was sick and she wanted to write a letter to cheer him up. But she didn't exactly know what to say to a child. She smoothed a new sheet of paper on her desk and tried again. This time she drew four playful rabbits and wrote: "My dear Noel, I don't know what to write to you, so I shall tell you a story about four little rabbits whose names were Flopsy, Mopsy, Cottontail and Peter..."

It was the first of many illustrated letters that Beatrix sent to Noel Moore and his siblings. With each letter, Beatrix added to the story. The children saved every single one—and it's a good thing they did. The letters sparked an idea that would make Beatrix one of the most celebrated children's authors of the twentieth century. And while she's most famous for creating Peter Rabbit and his friends, Beatrix Potter was also a naturalist, a hardworking farmer, and one of England's first conservationists.

Naturally Curious

In 1866 Beatrix Potter was born in a tall brick house in London. She spent her childhood in the third-floor nursery, learning languages with a governess and reading books like *Alice's Adventures in Wonderland*. Beatrix wasn't allowed to attend school, and her strict mother refused to let her play with other children. Helen Potter feared that other children's germs would make her family sick. Without her little brother, Bertram, and their menagerie of pets, Beatrix would have been a very lonely child.

Even though she was born in an exciting city, Beatrix always believed she belonged somewhere else: a green leafy place with no buildings or smog to blot out the sky. Every summer, the Potter family rented a house in the countryside. There, Beatrix's parents relaxed their strict rules, and she explored the outdoors with her sketchbook. She drew mushrooms that sprouted from tree stumps and wildflowers that waved in the breeze.

More than anything, Beatrix drew animals, especially her pets: a dog named Spot, Punch the frog, Toby the lizard, a white rat named Sammy, along with a falcon, owl, snake, bat, some squirrels, mice, and rabbits. Beatrix drew realistic nature sketches but she often added her own imaginative flourishes. Sometimes she couldn't help adding a scarf to a mouse or a jacket to a rabbit. Even her parents' friends—a group of artists and naturalists—could see that young Beatrix had a rare talent.

But talent or not, Beatrix's future was decided. Like most wealthy British women of her time, unless she got married she couldn't do anything without her parents' approval or even move out of the family home. As a young woman, Beatrix spent most of her time taking care of her parents and pursuing her hobbies: painting and studying natural history, paleontology, and mycology (the study of fungi). Without a university degree or the freedom to work, however, each path led to a dead end—until her art opened a door.

One day, Beatrix's friend Anne Moore suggested that Beatrix write a book using the illustrated letters she had written to Anne's children. Beatrix self-published *The Tale of Peter Rabbit* in 1901 when she was thirty-five years old. The mischievous main character was based on her pet rabbit, who according to Beatrix was "a noisy, cheerful, determined animal, inclined to attack strangers." A few months later, a London publishing house printed a revised, color version of *The Tale of Peter Rabbit*. The book was an instant hit.

Beatrix and her new publisher planned more illustrated animal books. She always drew from real life, using her pets as models. Beatrix based her next book, *The Tale of Squirrel Nutkin*, on her pet squirrel. For *The Tailor of Gloucester*, she let mice roam free in a dollhouse so she could sketch the way they climbed onto doll-sized chairs or poked their heads into tiny cupboards. And *The Tale of Mrs. Tiggy-Winkle* was based on Beatrix's pet hedgehog, Mrs. Tiggy. For a time, things were looking up for Beatrix. She had books to write and illustrate, she was earning her own money at last, and she became engaged to her publisher, Norman Warne.

Then things took an unexpectedly sad turn. Norman died suddenly of leukemia and Beatrix was left alone. Yet even in her grief, she was determined to make a new start. In 1905, Beatrix bought a farm in England's Lake District, where she had spent summers as a teenager. At first, Beatrix could only stay at the property, known as Hill Top Farm, for a few weeks a year, but she leased the land to a farmer and soon bought sheep, cows, ducks, hens, and beehives. Beatrix's next few books were inspired by the sights and sounds of Hill Top Farm.

Loving the Land

As the new century marched on, big changes came to the English countryside. Traditional farming methods were being replaced by machines, and the landscape was threatened by industrial projects like railroads and dams. Some people thought these changes signaled progress, but not Beatrix. She thought the countryside was special, not only the woodlands, fells, and lakes but also the rural way of life. When Beatrix moved to Hill Top Farm full-time, she made it her mission to protect the wild beauty of the Lake District and its rural community. Using the income from her books, she spent the next few years buying land. Eventually, Beatrix owned more than 4,000 acres of forests, lakes, and hills, including fifteen working farms.

When she was forty-seven years old, Beatrix married William Heelis, a local lawyer. The two spent the rest of their lives raising prize-winning sheep, working on their farms, and preserving the countryside. Beatrix wrote and illustrated thirty-three children's books and became famous throughout the world, but most of her neighbors simply knew her as a fellow farmer. When Beatrix died at age seventy-seven, she gave her farms and property to the British people by donating them to the National Trust, an organization that preserves places with natural beauty or historical importance. Today the land Beatrix loved and protected is part of Lake District National Park, a place that continues to inspire artists and travelers, support farmers, and preserve an awe-inspiring landscape.

AMAZING
ANIMAL COMMUNITIES

Humans aren't the only animals who have parents, learn from their aunts and uncles, play with their siblings, or belong to a family. Many animals depend on other members of their species for protection, food, knowledge, even friendship. After all, bees live in hives, ants work together in colonies, and birds migrate in flocks. But mammals have especially strong and complex **COMMUNITIES**. Biologists think this is one of the reasons mammals thrive in a variety of habitats.

Some animals are born ready to head into the world on their own. Consider baby sea turtles, who never meet their parents at all. They hatch from their shells on the shore and head straight to the ocean. But newborn mammals are pretty helpless and need time to grow and learn. That's why mammals stay with their families for a few months, years—or even their whole lives. Consider these fascinating mammal families:

African Elephants

Baby African elephants grow up in a herd of cousins and older female relatives (called *cows*) including their mothers, aunts, and grandmothers. The leader of the herd is the oldest female elephant. She shows the others where to find food and water, teaches younger females how to be mothers, and keeps a careful eye on the herd's young members. Older male elephants (called *bulls*) usually live alone or in groups with other bulls.

Meerkats

Meerkats have a reputation for being social. They live in large, energetic groups called *mobs* that can include up to thirty meerkats from different families. Mothers, fathers, and siblings all help raise the younger pups. One of the biggest advantages of this community is safety. Meerkats take turns watching for predators like snakes and hawks and alert the group when danger is near.

Wolves

Wolves live in families called *packs*. There are two leaders—a male wolf and a female wolf—and the rest are usually the pair's offspring. Wolves often stay with their family for their entire lives, but they can also start a new pack by having pups of their own. Similar to dogs, wolves communicate with one another by using body language and by growling, whining, and howling. Different howls have different meanings. There's even a special howl that wolves use when they're lost so the pack can find them.

Hyenas

Hyenas are misunderstood animals. People often think they're dangerous, dirty scavengers. But wildlife biologists say that hyenas are smart hunters and protective parents who play with their offspring more than any other carnivore. Each of the four hyena species lives in clans. The clans are led by females (who are larger and more aggressive than the males) and can include up to one hundred members. Hyenas spend their days in smaller groups, but when they need to hunt or defend their territory, the clan comes together.

Bonobos

Bonobos are cousins of chimpanzees. But because of their smaller population and limited habitat, these endangered primates are not as well-known as chimps. Like other primates, bonobos are very social. They live in groups of thirty to one hundred members that are led by females. Most younger females must leave the group when they grow up, but male bonobos stay with their mothers their whole lives. Bonobos are the most peaceful of the great apes. They'll help or share food with not only their own group members but strangers too.

Lions

Lions are the most social of all wild felines. In fact, they are the only big cat that lives in large family groups. These groups are called *prides*, and they include many related female lions who hunt and raise their cubs together. A pride can have as many as forty individuals, including adult females, cubs, and a few adult males.

WATCH FOR WILDLIFE

Whether you live in a suburb, a downtown neighborhood, or in the country, you likely have wildlife neighbors. Birds and insects are often easier to spot, but if you know where and how to look, you can see mammals too. Here are some ways to discover which animals live near you.

WAIT AND SEE. If you want to see wildlife, it's best to watch for it near sunset. Mammals can be *diurnal* (active during the day), *nocturnal* (active at night), and *crepuscular* (most active at twilight). Common North American animals like deer, raccoons, and squirrels are crepuscular. Choose an outdoor spot near a place where animals might like to be, such as water or trees. Sit quietly and see who shows up!

INVESTIGATE WILDLIFE CLUES. Animals almost always leave behind evidence. Look for animal tracks in soft dirt, mud, or snow. But tracks aren't the only clues. You can also identify animals by their scat (aka poop), like biologists do. Scat can provide information about animals such as what they've eaten and how healthy they are. (Just be sure to only look at scat—don't touch it!) Use the following pictures of common North American mammal tracks and match them to the tracks you find. You can also use an app like MyNature Animal Tracks to see photos of tracks and scat.

 WHITE-TAILED DEER

 PORCUPINE

 RACCOON

 SKUNK

 OPOSSUM

 FOX

 GRAY SQUIRREL

 COYOTE

 EASTERN COTTONTAIL RABBIT

SPOT THEIR HOMES. Animal homes can be hidden or out in the open. If you see one, keep a respectful distance so you don't disturb the animal. Here are some common North American animal homes:

- Beaver lodge

- Muskrat push-up

- Ground squirrel burrow

- Squirrel nest

- Fox den

LEARN THEIR SOUNDS. Just like birds, you can identify mammals by their sounds or calls. Squirrels chatter, raccoons whine, beavers slap their tails, and gophers squeak.

CHINA'S GIANT PANDAS

In 1936, a new animal arrived at Chicago's Brookfield Zoo that few people outside central China had ever seen. It was a furry bear that reminded people of a raccoon. Unlike other bears, however, this animal didn't use its sharp teeth to eat meat or berries but instead munched only on leaves. It was called a **GIANT PANDA** and it had been smuggled out of China and sold to the zoo. Over the next few decades, many more giant pandas were taken from the wild and sold—or sometimes given as gifts from the Chinese government—to zoos around the world.

Biologists learned a lot about giant pandas (usually shortened to "pandas") from these captive animals. But when researchers finally studied the bears in the wild, they discovered that pandas and their habitat were in serious trouble. Pandas live only in China's central mountains and they need bamboo forests to survive—the plant makes up 99 percent of their diet. It's so low in nutrients that a panda eats nearly 40 pounds of bamboo every day! In the 1960s, China took the first step in protecting these animals by creating the first wildlife reserves to save their shrinking bamboo habitat.

But these few wildlife reserves weren't enough to save the panda. By the 1980s, half the panda's remaining habitat had been destroyed, and there were only about 1,000 wild pandas left. The giant panda was placed on a global endangered species list. With the help of the World Wildlife Fund, an international conservation group, China created even more nature reserves and research centers. But pandas weren't reproducing fast enough, so biologists also had to find a way to boost their population. After many years of research, scientists finally figured out how to breed pandas in captivity so they could release bears into the wild.

Since then, more than a hundred baby pandas have been born and raised at research centers in China. Some of these pandas remain in captivity, but at Wolong Panda Center, researchers teach cubs how to survive in the wild, then release them in wildlife reserves. (It's very important that these little pandas don't get used to humans. To make sure this doesn't happen, Wolong's researchers wear panda costumes!) In the early 2000s, panda conservation efforts began to pay off. In a single decade, panda habitat increased by 12 percent and the animal's population increased by 17 percent. There are now an estimated 1,850 wild pandas, and China is planning a national park that would combine several wildlife reserves and protect more habitat.

In 2016 the giant panda's conservation status was changed from "endangered" to "vulnerable." Plenty of challenges remain. The panda is still a rare animal and there are still threats to its habitat, including climate change. But the story of the panda shows that when people work together to tackle environmental challenges, endangered animals can be saved before it's too late.

WRITE AN
ANIMAL STORY

Books and screens are full of stories about animals. Sometimes the stories are true, or *nonfiction*, like this book. And sometimes they're made-up. But even fictional stories like Beatrix Potter's books or the latest animated movie are inspired by real animals. Beatrix might have imagined her famous rabbit wearing a coat and drinking tea, but she studied real animals that lived in the English countryside and used this information to create her books (see page 88). Writing a story about animals can be a fun way to learn more about them. By imagining how the world looks through their eyes, it helps you (and your readers!) understand them a bit better.

Write a fictional story about animals. It can be a picture book, novel, mystery, a story that rhymes, or a graphic novel. It might help to have some inspiration. Try writing a story that begins with one of the following sentences.

Story Starters:

- I never knew that animals could talk until the day I got lost in the woods.

- The fox waited until everyone else was asleep, and then she snuck outside to see for herself.

- The nest looked ordinary, except for the shiny purple egg. Was it *glowing*?

- Scientists thought the animal was extinct—until I found one in my backpack.

- Hedgehogs can't fly. But that didn't stop Felix from trying.

CHRISTIAN

THE LION WHO RETURNED TO THE WILD

A department store is no place for a lion. That's what John Rendell and Ace Bourke thought when they saw a lion cub in a too-small cage at Harrods department store. It was 1969, and because the United Kingdom had not yet passed wildlife protection laws, some stores sold wild animals as pets. John and Ace lived in a small flat in downtown London, but they thought they could give the lion a better home.

The friends named the lion Christian and he went everywhere with them. He was as affectionate as a housecat. Yet as the lion grew, he couldn't continue living in a city. John and Ace met people who agreed to return Christian to the wild: actors and activists Bill Travers and Virginia McKenna and wildlife conservationist George Adamson. In 1970 they brought Christian to Kora National Park in Kenya.

One year later, John and Ace visited the reserve. Christian was now an adult and the leader of a pride. No one knew what to expect when the three were reunited. As Bill Travers filmed, Christian approached John and Ace. Then he playfully jumped up, hugging and nuzzling the men like a kitten. Christian's story—and the amazing reunion—was later featured in several documentaries and books. Forty years later, a video of the reunion went viral on social media, introducing a new generation to "the hugging lion" and his incredible bond with the two men who helped set him free.

THE WILDLIFE ADVOCATE
GEORGE MELÉNDEZ WRIGHT

JUNE 20, 1904–FEBRUARY 25, 1936

"The unique charm of the animals in a national park
lies in their wildness, not their tameness."

—George Meléndez Wright

As dusk fell in the national park, an excited crowd gathered to watch the evening program. They climbed the wooden bleachers, then blinked as the spotlights illuminated a platform covered with trash and food scraps: bear food. As the audience watched, bears wandered in from the forest, following their noses to the makeshift stage. A few black bears arrived first, then a few more. Even a grizzly showed up.

The curious crowd sat only a few feet from the powerful (and hungry) animals. A young naturalist named George Meléndez Wright shifted in his seat. The spectacle made him uncomfortable. George was a scientist who was studying the U.S. national parks' wildlife. He thought bears and other animals should be respected as wild creatures, not treated as tame pets to entertain tourists. George's ideas weren't popular then, but one day, they would be.

The Young Naturalist

In the 1920s, people visited U.S. national parks for some of the same reasons they do today: beautiful scenery, outdoor adventure, fresh air, and wildlife watching. But their attitudes and behaviors were different, especially when it came to the parks' animal residents. Wildlife was often seen as entertainment. Public bear feedings were a common sight, tourists were encouraged to feed wildlife (sometimes from their car windows), and parks had small zoos where they'd display local animals like mountain lions and bison. But not all animals were welcome in the parks. Predators like wolves and coyotes—even pelicans—were killed by park rangers to preserve animals such as deer and fish, which attracted hunters and anglers to the parks. Science didn't play a part in park decisions about animals—until naturalists like George came along.

George Meléndez Wright was born in San Francisco in 1904. His father was a wealthy ship captain and his mother was an immigrant from an influential family in El Salvador. Sadly, both of George's parents died when he was young.

His two older brothers were adopted by relatives in El Salvador and George was adopted by a great-aunt in San Francisco. From an early age, George's aunt encouraged her nephew's love of the outdoors. When he was still a teenager, he backpacked alone along the California coast, taught natural history at a Boy Scouts camp, and was president of his high school's Audubon Society. In 1920, when he was just sixteen years old, George enrolled in the University of California, Berkeley to study forestry and zoology.

Rewilding Animals

After graduation, George got a job with the National Park Service as an assistant naturalist. Although he was young and inexperienced, he had big, bold ideas. As a zoologist, George believed that part of the national parks' mission should be to preserve wildlife in their natural habitats. He was frustrated with the way animals were treated in the parks and dismayed by the destruction of their habitat due to ranching and commercial development. But George needed information to back up his ideas if he wanted other people to listen. George asked his supervisors if he could conduct a scientific survey of all the wildlife in the national parks. No one had ever done anything like it. It took a year to get his supervisor's approval, and in the end, George used his own money to pay for the project.

In 1930, George set out with two colleagues to tour the national parks of the western U.S. Over the next few years, George traveled 11,000 miles as he visited fourteen national parks. At each stop, he recorded the animals he saw and interviewed park staff, ranchers, and hunters about their experiences with wildlife. He saw firsthand how park policies were having negative effects on animals and their habitats, and he began to speak out against practices like feeding bears and keeping wild bison in corrals for tourists' entertainment.

George published his findings in a groundbreaking two-part study called *Fauna of the National Parks of the United States*. In it, George shared his data and advocated for science-based management of wildlife. He outlined practices like letting predators control prey populations, no longer allowing tourists to feed wildlife, and restoring habitats. The report concluded with twenty recommendations for new park policies. Some people resisted George's ideas, but his outgoing personality and sound science helped win support for his vision. A year after his report was published, George's recommendations became official park policy. Then in 1933, George was named head of the National Park Service's first Wildlife Division.

In 1936, however, George's important work was tragically cut short. He died in a car accident, leaving behind his wife and two daughters. Although George was only thirty-two years old, the work he did in his short time with the National Park Service had a lasting influence on its people, policies, lands, and wildlife. Today George is honored as the founder of science-based wildlife management in the national parks, and visitors can see animals the way he once envisioned:
wild and free.

WAYS TO CARE

YOU: Create Animal Habitat

Habitat destruction is one of the biggest threats to wildlife. And while it's critical to protect large ecosystems like rainforests, small habitats matter too. Protecting an entire species can start with helping a few individual animals. Here are some habitats you can create to help animals near you:

Build a bat house. Bats are the only true flying mammal. They have an unfortunate reputation for being scary, but they're helpful creatures who control insect populations, pollinate flowers, and spread seeds. As nocturnal animals, they need a safe place to roost during the day. You can build or buy a bat house to give your neighborhood bats a place to live.

Make a squirrel nest box. Squirrels usually nest in hollow trees or use dead leaves to build nests called *dreys*. You can give them another place to live by building or buying a squirrel nest box.

Plant a shrub. Small mammals like rabbits and mice depend on shrubs for shelter. Planting a shrub or two in your yard is an easy way to create animal habitat for small mammals.

LOCAL: Help Wildlife Rehabilitators

Wildlife rehabilitation centers care for orphaned and injured wildlife until they can be released back into the wild. Most of the time wildlife rehabilitators work with adult volunteers, but there are still ways kids can help. You may be able to organize a donation drive to collect supplies or hold a fundraiser for the center. Ask an adult to help you find a wildlife rehabilitation center in your area and ask how you can help. (Learn more about wildlife rehabilitators on page 174.)

GLOBAL: Speak Up About the Wildlife Trade

In the past, people kept wild animals like crocodiles and chimpanzees as pets and thought nothing of it. But now we know how harmful this is not only for the animals but for the whole world. Sadly, millions of wild animals are captured each year for their meat, fur, shells, horns—and they're also sold as pets. The wildlife trade hurts animals and their populations, changes ecosystems, and spreads disease among humans and other animals. One way to protect wildlife is to teach others about why it's important to keep wildlife wild. Here are some ways to do that:

- Give a presentation to your class.

- Start a school club for students who are interested in protecting wildlife.

- Create art that you can share in person or online.

- Support or volunteer with an organization that helps wildlife around the world, like Earth Rangers, Roots and Shoots, or the World Wildlife Fund.

Save Our Wildlife!

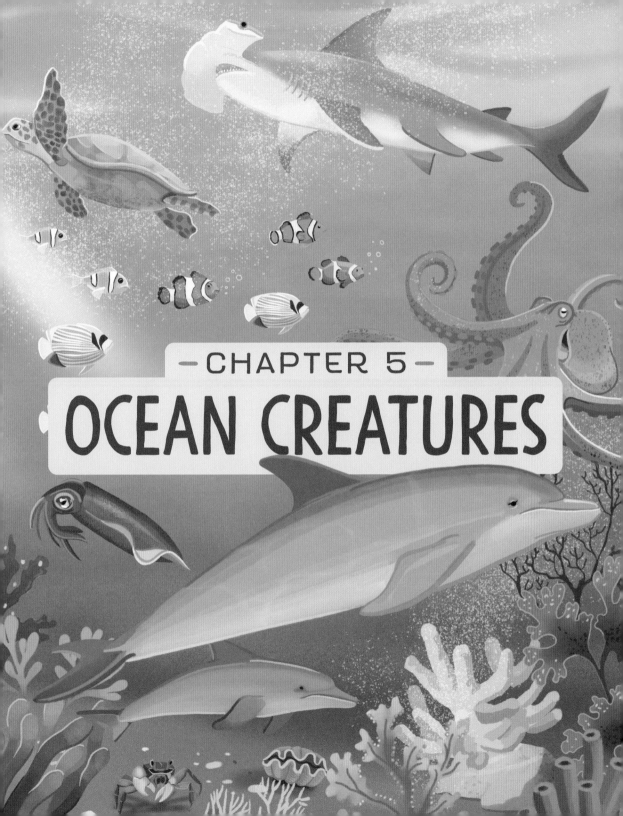

-CHAPTER 5-
OCEAN CREATURES

The ocean is full of animal life. Scientists can't even say for sure how many marine animal species there are. (They estimate more than one million!) And the diversity of creatures that swim and float in the Earth's saltwater is astounding. There are familiar mammals like the playful dolphin and shy manatee. Mollusks like clams and octopus. Seabirds and reptiles like penguins and sea turtles. And of course, fish: schools of shiny blue tuna, prowling sharks, and colorful clownfish. Animals who live in the ocean often seem more different from each other than alike, but they have at least one thing in common: all depend on a healthy, vibrant ocean to thrive.

⋙ OCEAN CREATURES FACTS ⋘

1. The ocean is home to both the biggest *and* smallest animals in the world. The **BLUE WHALE** is the biggest, measuring up to 100 feet long and weighing about 190 tons. (That's about the weight of 30 African elephants, the largest land animal.) The smallest marine animals are **ZOOPLANKTON**, microscopic creatures that are the base of the entire ocean's food chain.

2. **95 PERCENT** of ocean animals are *invertebrates*, animals who don't have a backbone. Clams, oysters, scallops, snails, slugs, octopus, and squid are all invertebrates.

3. Sight and smell are limited underwater, so many marine animals depend on **SOUND** to communicate and navigate. Whales and dolphins make calls and clicks. Certain fish can grunt or growl, and crabs and shrimp click or tap their claws.

4. Animals who live in the darkest, deepest parts of the ocean **GLOW IN THE DARK**! Scientists call this *bioluminescence*; it's the result of a chemical reaction that happens in the animals' bodies. Most of the time, bioluminescent animals appear to glow in shades of blue and green.

BIOGRAPHY

THE SHARK SCIENTIST
DR. EUGENIE CLARK

MAY 4, 1922–FEBRUARY 25, 2015

"I don't think I ever consciously wanted to be an explorer. I didn't know what
an explorer was. I just knew that I wanted to study fish."

—Dr. Eugenie Clark

Eugenie saw her very first shark in an unlikely place: Manhattan. The nine-year-old girl pressed her face against the aquarium glass and stared into an unfamiliar underwater world. She was captivated by all the swimming creatures but she especially loved sharks, with their streamlined bodies and sharp fins that cut through the water like blades. Eugenie wondered how fast the sharks could swim if they were in the ocean and not in a New York City aquarium. She wished she could see that sight for herself—maybe wearing a diving suit and helmet, swimming above the seafloor like her hero, biologist William Beebe.

Eugenie had always loved the sea. She learned to swim by the time she was two and took many childhood trips to the beach. Her mother, Yumico, and her stepfather, Masatomo Nobu, were from Japan. Because Japan is a country of islands, the ocean plays an important part in its culture, history, and food. Her stepfather owned a Japanese restaurant in New York City and Eugenie grew up eating seafood: rice and nori (dried seaweed) for breakfast and dishes made with raw fish, octopus, and sea urchin eggs. At a young age, she already knew more about the ocean than her classmates.

But Eugenie's first look at ocean life underwater was at the New York Aquarium in 1931. On Saturdays, while her mother worked at a nearby newsstand, Eugenie wandered the aquarium, marveling at the tropical fish and powerful sharks. She wondered: *What if I could spend the rest of my life studying fish in the ocean?* Eugenie didn't waste time getting started. Her mother bought her a 15-gallon aquarium filled with fish. Then Eugenie read all the books she could about ocean creatures and learned there was a name for a scientist who studied fish: an *ichthyologist.*

In the 1930s, there weren't many women scientists and women were often discouraged from even *studying* science. When Eugenie told her parents she wanted to be a biologist like William Beebe, they told her that if she studied hard, maybe she could be a secretary for someone like him. But Eugenie insisted. No, she would study the ocean and see its wonders for herself.

Studying Sharks

Eugenie's first step was to study at a university, and in 1942 she graduated from Hunter College with a degree in zoology. Then she worked as a researcher in California at the Scripps Institution of Oceanography. In a class of thirty-five graduate students, Eugenie was one of only two women. On a research trip to Palau in the Pacific Ocean, Eugenie was floating near a coral reef when she saw a shark in the wild for the first time. "Seen in their own environment, sharks are incredibly beautiful," Eugenie later said. The 8-foot shark slowly swam by, paying no attention to the awestruck diver.

In 1953, Eugenie wrote a best-selling book about her ocean adventures and research called *Lady with a Spear*. A couple named William and Anne Vanderbilt read Eugenie's book and saw how popular her lectures were when she spoke to Florida audiences about local marine life. The Vanderbilts suggested she start a small marine research lab in Florida and offered to pay for it. Eugenie did just that and in 1955 she became the founding director of Cape Haze Marine Laboratory, a rare accomplishment for a woman at that time.

At Cape Haze, Eugenie conducted groundbreaking experiments on shark behavior and intelligence. Before Eugenie's experiments, most people assumed that sharks were not smart; that's why her findings surprised Eugenie *and* the rest of the world. One of her experiments showed that sharks could be taught to ring a bell for their meals by pushing a button. "The more we study sharks, the more we realize that we have underestimated their capabilities," Eugenie said. In 1967 the lab's name was changed to Mote Marine Laboratory, and eventually it became a world-class marine research lab. It now has more than 200 staff members and 1,400 volunteers who research all aspects of the ocean, including coral reef restoration, sea turtle conservation, and medical research.

Underwater Adventures

Eugenie spent the rest of her long career studying fish and sharks all over the world. Although she never set out to be an explorer, that's what she became. She pioneered the use of scuba gear in underwater research, and she led more than two hundred expeditions to places like Mexico, Japan, Palau, Thailand, Indonesia, the Caribbean, and the Red Sea. She traveled to the ocean's depths, conducting seventy-two dives using submersibles. In her journeys, Eugenie studied fish species that had never been seen in their natural habitats and discovered new species too—some were even named after her.

Eugenie also spent her life teaching others about marine animals and conservation *and* dispelling myths about sharks. Sharks never had a good reputation, but it got even worse in the 1970s when a popular book and movie portrayed them as ruthless monsters that attacked people. In truth, few of the more than 400 shark species would attack a human. "No creature on earth has a worse, and perhaps less deserved, reputation than the shark," Eugenie once wrote. In all her years swimming among sharks, Eugenie was bitten only once—by a tiny newborn tiger shark!

When Eugenie died at the age of ninety-two in 2015, she was still diving, writing, and researching marine animals. She was just as excited and curious as the nine-year-old girl who first visited the aquarium and imagined a life spent under the sea.

INCREDIBLE
OCEAN JOURNEYS

For many ocean animals, life is a literal **JOURNEY**—a continual voyage from one part of the ocean to another. In a watery world that's pushed and pulled by tides, shaped by powerful currents, and churned up by waves, it's often easier to go with the flow. While some ocean creatures stay in one place for their whole lives, most travel to find food, warmer or cooler temperatures, a mate, or a safe place to raise their young. And because of climate change, more animals than ever are on the move. Over 80 percent of ocean animals are changing where and how they migrate because of the rising ocean temperature. This could have lasting effects on ecosystems, especially the ocean food chain.

Sometimes marine journeys are short. For instance, each night animals who live in the deepest parts of the ocean rise to the surface to feed. In this *vertical migration*, animals like squid may travel thousands of feet up to their feeding grounds. But often, a marine animal's migration is long, slow, and full of potential danger.

Humpback Whales

All whale species migrate, but the humpback whale travels the farthest. Humpbacks spend summer feeding in polar waters and then travel thousands of miles to the subtropics or tropics, where they give birth and raise their calves. Some humpbacks will swim 5,000 miles from one point to the other—without ever stopping to eat.

Spiny Lobsters

These crustaceans live in subtropical and tropical areas around the world. They lay their eggs in warm, shallow water and then migrate to deeper water by walking along the ocean floor. But they don't do it alone. Spiny lobsters are known to migrate in a single-file line. The lines can be up to fifty lobsters long!

Freshwater Eels

Freshwater eels are born in the distant Sargasso Sea, a calm region of the Atlantic Ocean. As soon as the eels hatch, they start traveling to the mouths of freshwater rivers thousands of miles away. Drifting along on the ocean's powerful currents, it can take these young eels up to two years to complete their journey.

Arctic Terns

The Arctic tern may spend a lot of its time in the sky, but as a seabird, it depends on the ocean to survive. This black-and-gray bird is the record holder for longest animal migration. Each year, it flies from the North Pole to the South Pole—and back again! It's estimated that Arctic terns fly more than 25,000 miles a year.

FUNGIE
THE DOLPHIN WHO BEFRIENDED PEOPLE

I n the winter of 1983, a lighthouse keeper named Paddy Ferriter on Ireland's Dingle Peninsula spotted a lone dolphin in the steel-gray surf. Dolphins are a common sight in those chilly Atlantic waters, but this dolphin's behavior set him apart. Paddy noticed that the dolphin followed the town's fishing boats out of the harbor each day, and over the next few years, the dolphin seemed to make its home in the harbor, leaping alongside boats and sometimes joining swimmers in the waves. People named the dolphin Fungie after a local fisherman. It's unusual for wild dolphins to stay in one small territory and even more unusual for them to regularly seek out humans. But that's what Fungie did—for the next thirty-seven years!

Before Fungie arrived, Dingle was a small, sleepy fishing village where jobs were growing scarce. But when word spread of their remarkable dolphin resident, people from all over the world came to Dingle. The little town became a tourist destination and business boomed. Fungie was shy at first, but as he grew used to his human audience, he became a playful (and sometimes mischievous) companion to fishing vessels, tour boats, and kayakers. He showed up nearly every day in the harbor, as predictable as the tide itself. Scientists could never say for certain why he seemed to prefer people to other dolphins. In many ways, the familiar dolphin remained a mystery.

In October 2020, Fungie disappeared. Dingle residents watched the waves for weeks for a sign of their beloved dolphin. But they knew Fungie was old for his species, at least forty, and he had likely died from old age. In fact, in 2019 *The Guinness Book of World Records* recognized him as the world's oldest solitary wild dolphin. Fungie may be gone, but he forever changed a small Irish town and the lives of countless people who witnessed the wonder of a wild dolphin.

THINK LIKE A
MARINE BIOLOGIST

A marine biologist is a scientist who studies ocean organisms and habitats. (The word *marine* comes from the Latin word *mare*, which means "sea.") To learn more about ocean creatures, try thinking and exploring like a marine biologist.

Choose a marine animal category to investigate.

- ☐ sharks
- ☐ zooplankton
- ☐ sea turtles
- ☐ seals or sea lions
- ☐ corals
- ☐ whales

- ☐ clams/mussels/
  oysters
- ☐ fish
- ☐ seabirds
- ☐ rays
- ☐ octopus or squid

- ☐ dolphins
- ☐ crabs/lobsters
- ☐ manatees
- ☐ other

Pick a species within that category. Some categories have more
species than others. For instance, there are over 400 shark species, but just
3 species of manatee.

Observe the animal in its habitat. If you live near the ocean or plan to
travel there, can you see this animal in the wild? If not, does this animal live at
an aquarium or zoo you can visit? If you can't see this animal in person, you
can observe it in its habitat by watching a video or nature documentary.

Answer the following questions using information from books, websites, or videos or by watching the animal in its habitat.

1. What's the name of the animal species?

2. What does the animal look like?

3. What animal family does it belong to?

4. Where does it live in the world?

5. What type of ocean environment does it live in?

6. What does it eat?

7. Is the animal's global population increasing, stable, or decreasing?

8. What are ways that humans have hurt this animal species?

9. What are ways that humans have helped this animal species?

10. What role does this animal play in its ecosystem?

Share what you've learned. Choose one of the following ways to share your findings:

☐ Create a book about the animal that includes facts, drawings, and photos.

☐ Record a podcast and talk about the animal or have a friend interview you.

☐ Build a model of the animal and its habitat, and use it for a class project or to teach your friends. You can use clay, Legos, or recycled items like cardboard for building materials.

SEA OTTERS
OF THE NORTH PACIFIC

A long the Pacific Coast, emerald-green forests grow beneath the ocean waves. Like forests that grow on land, they're home to countless animals. But in these underwater worlds, the "trees" are kelp, a type of algae that can grow to 100 feet tall. And instead of bears or wolves, a different furry animal prowls and plays in this leafy maze: **SEA OTTERS**. Sea otters are called the keepers of the kelp forest because this special ecosystem wouldn't exist without them.

Three hundred years ago, more than 200,000 sea otters lived along the North Pacific coasts from southern California to Russia. But in the 1700s traders discovered that beaver, mink, and otter furs were warm and useful and could be sold for a lot of money. Sea otter hunting was rampant until 1911, when it was banned internationally. By then nearly all the North Pacific's sea otters had been killed for their fur, and they'd disappeared from the west coast of North America. Or so it seemed.

One day in the early twentieth century, a group of sea otters was spotted off the California coast. To protect the animals, the California Department of Fish and Wildlife kept them a secret for the next twenty years. When the public finally learned of their existence, many people were thrilled to see the animals return—but not everyone. Sea otters eat sea urchins and mollusks like clams and abalones. With the sea otters gone, shellfish populations had exploded and become profitable for commercial fisheries. Though scientific evidence didn't support their claims, abalone fishermen blamed sea otters for hurting their business, and they opposed early conservation efforts to protect the species.

Margaret Ownings was an artist and environmentalist who was determined to protect sea otters. In 1968, she founded a conservation organization called Friends of the Sea Otter. Over the next several decades, Margaret and other conservationists worked to protect the sea otter and its habitat. They campaigned for new environmental laws and supported scientific research that helped people better understand the sea otter. Over time, California's sea otter population grew to 3,200.

We now know that sea otters aren't pests or an endless supply of furs. They're a *keystone species*, which is a species that's critical to the health of its ecosystem. Sea otters control the population of marine animals such as sea urchins that would otherwise destroy the biodiversity of the kelp forests. And coastal communities have discovered that sea otters are good for their local economies. Today the tourism industry near sea otter habitat is more profitable than the shellfish industry ever was. And the good news extends beyond California: thanks to decades of conservation work, the global sea otter population has risen from barely 1,000 to 125,000, and they've finally returned to most of their home range along the North Pacific coasts.

SCULPT A CORAL REEF

Coral reefs are known for their beautiful colors and eye-catching shapes. But they're more than underwater sculptures. They're habitats that support animal life. And even more incredible? Corals are animals too. They look like stone or plants, but coral reefs are made up of tiny animals called *polyps*.

You can create a coral reef sculpture using clay. You'll need air-dry clay in several colors and tools to shape the clay (pencils, toothpicks, plastic butter-knife, etc.) Start by making the base of your reef. Roll some clay into a ball that's slightly smaller than a tennis ball. Flatten the bottom of the ball by pressing it against a tabletop so it looks like a small mound. Create a rough texture across the mound by poking small holes with a pencil. Next, make corals based on photos, your imagination, or the ideas on the following page.

1. Tube Coral

Roll 5 or more small clay logs and pinch them together at one end. Use a pencil to poke a hole in the end of each log and twist it a little so the logs become tubes.

2. Lettuce Coral

Roll a small log that's about 3 inches long, then flatten it. Starting at one end, fold up the clay accordion-style until you reach the other end. Pinch the bottom together so the folds fan out.

3. Pillar Coral

Make several thin logs that are pointed at one end. With the pointed ends up, bunch the logs together at the nonpointed end.

4. Sea Anemone

Roll 9 to 12 very thin logs. Pinch them together at one end.

5. Table Coral

Roll a small ball of clay about the size of a pea. Flatten the ball, then dot the surface with holes using a pencil. Peel up the clay and use your fingers to make the edges a little wavy.

Immediately after making your corals, attach them to the coral reef base. Use a plastic butter knife to make a few faint lines in the bottom of each coral piece and the place where you will attach it to the base. Dip your finger in water and dab both places. Then press the coral piece onto the base. Repeat with the other corals. Let the reef air-dry for at least 24 hours. If any of the pieces don't stay attached, you can attach them with craft glue once the clay has dried.

BIOGRAPHY

THE MANATEE RESCUER
JAMAL GALVES

BORN DECEMBER 16, 1986

"Manatees are very important to my life. It's not a job to me. I felt it was my duty to speak up for these animals that can't speak for themselves. Just because they can't speak doesn't mean that they don't have something to say."

—Jamal Galves

As long as humans have sailed the seas, they have told tales of mysterious ocean creatures like kraken, sea serpents, and elusive mermaids. In 1493, as Christopher Columbus sailed the Caribbean, he spotted three unfamiliar creatures swimming in the turquoise waves. The animals didn't have dorsal fins, so they couldn't be dolphins or sharks. When the gray curves of their tails broke the water's surface, Columbus realized what he was seeing: mermaids! He recorded the sighting in his journal, adding a note that the creatures were less beautiful than he'd expected, especially their faces. But like so many sailors and seafarers throughout history, Columbus was mistaken. The creatures weren't mermaids *or* sea monsters—they were manatees.

Life Among Manatees

Jamal Galves didn't grow up hearing legends about manatees; he saw them with his own eyes nearly every day. Jamal was born in 1986 and grew up in a small coastal village in Belize named Gales Point Manatee. Next to the warm Caribbean Sea and threaded with lagoons and rivers, Jamal's village is known for its large population of manatees. Manatees are large mammals that live in both saltwater and freshwater. They have tough gray skin like an elephant and flippers like a dolphin. They're called "sea cows" because just like the familiar farm animal, manatees are gentle and slow-moving and spend most of their days grazing. (Though in the manatees' case, they graze on seagrass and other underwater plants.)

Jamal watched the manatees at his neighborhood docks as often as he could. Sometimes he and his cousins played together in their grandmother's yard, pretending to be manatee rescuers. But Jamal didn't have to wait long to help real manatees. When he was twelve years old, he spotted a group of scientists boarding a boat. He didn't know it at the time, but the group was led by Dr. James Powell, a well-known biologist and manatee conservationist. Jamal boldly asked Dr. Powell if he could join the researchers on their trip that day. The biologist hesitated at first—there weren't any other kids on the trip—but then he welcomed Jamal aboard.

That day on the boat was a turning point in Jamal's life. He saw a manatee up close and out of the water for the first time, as he helped the scientists pull manatees on board to perform health assessments. He learned that manatees were endangered and that their main threats came from humans. Manatees around the world were being hurt or killed by boat collisions and discarded fishing gear, and their habitats were being destroyed by water pollution.

When Jamal heard these sad stories, he wanted to do something right away. "Why not me? Why can't I be that person that's going to save this species?" he wondered. He didn't wait until he was older to start making a difference. From then on, Jamal volunteered with the research team every year, helping to monitor, track, and rehabilitate manatees. When he turned sixteen, he was officially offered a job with the research team.

A Conservation Leader

Today Jamal is a conservation biologist for the Clearwater Marine Aquarium's Research Institute, and he's the program coordinator for their manatee research program in Belize. He's dedicated to saving the endangered Antillean manatee, the subspecies that swims in the waters around Belize. Fewer than 2,500 Antillean manatees remain in the wild, and there's still a lot to learn about this rare species, which keeps Jamal motivated. He spends every day helping these manatees in some way. Sometimes he's on the water monitoring local populations or releasing a rehabilitated manatee back into the ocean. Other days, he's rescuing orphaned manatee calves or teaching students— from kindergarten to college—about conservation. "You're never too young to start saving a species," Jamal says.

Jamal's work has changed people's minds about this shy marine animal, and he's gathered data that the Belize government uses to create marine sanctuaries and catch poachers. In recent years, he has been honored by National Geographic, World Wildlife Fund, and his country's government. But more than recognition, Jamal wants to share his knowledge and passion for manatees with younger generations, just as biologists like Dr. Powell once did with him. "My goal is to instill that [passion] in the next generation," Jamal says, "so that when I can no longer do this, there are people that continue the work, continue to ensure that these animals are safe for a lifetime."

WAYS TO CARE

YOU: Keep Seashells at the Seashore

Seashells are popular souvenirs all over the world. But that's a big problem, because shells are more than knickknacks. They come from living mollusks and other animals that keep our oceans vibrant and healthy, and harvesting shells to be sold in stores as souvenirs, jewelry, and home décor is hurting ocean ecosystems. One way to help the ocean—and people who depend on it for their livelihoods—is to stop buying shells and start buying products made from recycled ocean plastics. New companies are hiring people to "harvest" the ocean's plastic waste instead of the ocean's creatures. These businesses help clean up the ocean, provide jobs, and turn waste into useful and beautiful products.

LOCAL: Clean Up Waterways

Did you know you can help solve the ocean's trash problem even if you don't live near the ocean? That's because trash from rivers can eventually end up in the ocean. There are people dreaming up big solutions to this big problem (like machines that filter trash from rivers), but in the meantime, small consistent action can still help. "Adopt" a river by choosing a river or stream near you, gathering some friends, and commiting to a once-a-month trash cleanup of the area around the waterway. Track your progress over time by counting how much trash you collect, or take photos of your haul. (And for safety's sake, remember to bring an adult with you and stay out of the water.)

GLOBAL: Support an Ocean Animal Species

People around the world are working to save marine animals. Some organizations focus on all ocean life, whereas others focus on a specific species. If there's a certain animal that interests you, consider learning about (and supporting) an organization that's helping that animal.

Sea Otters: Defenders of Wildlife (defenders.org)

Whales: Save the Whales (savethewhales.org)

Sharks: Project AWARE (projectaware.org/sharks)

Oysters: Billion Oyster Project (billionoysterproject.org)

Sea Turtles: Sea Turtle Conservancy (conserveturtles.org)

Fish: Wild Oceans (wildoceans.org)

-CHAPTER 6-
FRESHWATER LIFE

When you think of freshwater animals, fish might be the first creatures that come to mind: speckled trout or silver minnows. But not all freshwater animals have fins or scales. They can also have wings or feathers or fur. And not all these animals live in the same type of watery habitat. Some creatures prefer quiet ponds where the water is warm and still. Others are at home in deep lakes or among the cattails that grow along lakeshores. The most tenacious creatures live in rivers or streams where the water is always moving and the environment constantly changes. Freshwater makes up only three percent of all water on earth, but nearly all life depends on it—especially the animals who live in and around it.

FRESHWATER LIFE FACTS

1. Freshwater habitats are home to **FISH**, **BIRDS**, **INSECTS**, **REPTILES**, **AMPHIBIANS**, **CRUSTACEANS**, **MOLLUSKS**, and **MAMMALS**.

2. Even animals who live underwater need **OXYGEN**. Some creatures, like snails, absorb oxygen through their skin. Others, like fish and water bugs, have gills or snorkels. And some animals, like water beetles, create air bubbles around their bodies before diving.

3. There are **MORE THAN 10,000** species of freshwater fish.

4. One of the world's largest fish is the endangered **BELUGA STURGEON**, which depends on the rivers that flow into the Caspian and Black Seas. The biggest beluga sturgeon ever recorded was more than 23 feet long and weighed more than 3,000 pounds.

5. Not many animals can live in loud, chaotic places like rushing streams or roaring waterfalls. Australia's **WATERFALL FROG** is one exception. Unlike most frogs, the waterfall frog doesn't call or sing. Its home is so loud, no one would hear it!

THE TURTLE TRAILBLAZER
TOMAS DIAGNE

BORN 1970

"I was not born a conservationist. I've become a conservationist. In the beginning, I wasn't interested in conservation, I was just interested in collecting turtles, having them, being next to them, watching them, and I started to learn: these species are declining."

—Tomas Diagne

Africa is a land of legendary wildlife. All across the continent, beautiful birds fill the skies, powerful predators like lions and cheetahs roam the plains, crocodiles snap their jaws, and monkeys gather in treetops. Scientists and tourists travel here from around the world for the chance to see magnificent animals in their natural habitats. With so many inspiring animal species and dramatic landscapes on one continent, it's easy to overlook less flashy creatures like Africa's turtles. And plenty of people do. That's one reason biologist Tomas Diagne has dedicated his life to studying and saving them.

Befriending Turtles

Tomas was born in Dakar, Senegal, in 1970. He grew up surrounded by animals but turtles were always his favorite. (*Turtles* is the common name for a group of reptiles that includes freshwater turtles, sea turtles, tortoises, and terrapins.) Whenever Tomas found wild turtles swimming in ponds or crawling through underbrush, he'd bring the reptiles to his father's farm on the outskirts of the city so he could study them more closely. There were plenty of other animals on the farm, so at first, it was easy for Tomas to hide a turtle or two indoors. But eventually, his collection got out of hand. "My house is not a zoo," his father said one day. He told Tomas to find somewhere else for the creatures to live—outdoors. Tomas did, but it wouldn't be the last time he studied turtles.

Senegal is a country on Africa's west coast. With a border on the Atlantic Ocean and a variety of habitats, it is home to several species of sea turtles, tortoises, and freshwater turtles. When Tomas was a child, few biologists studied Africa's turtles, especially the species that lived in West Africa. Most of the continent's wildlife research and conservation happened in eastern Africa. But when Tomas was a young man, he met biologists in his country who taught him the reptiles he admired were endangered *and* that he could do something about it.

Once Tomas understood what needed to be done to help Senegal's turtles, he was inspired to act. In 1992, when he was twenty-two years old, Tomas started his first nonprofit conservation organization to help sulcata tortoises, a local species and Africa's largest tortoise species. Sulcatas are endangered in their home range because of habitat destruction and the tortoise's popularity as a pet throughout the world. (Poachers capture wild sulcatas and sell them.) A year later, Tomas and his cousin Lamine Diagne founded Village des Tortues, Senegal's first sulcata tortoise rescue. Village des Tortues is still going strong today and now houses 300 tortoises.

Changing Minds

Saving the sulcata tortoise was just the beginning of Tomas's wildlife work. He later became one of the first biologists to specialize in Africa's turtles, discovering facts about their behaviors and habitats that no one else knew. He also led some of the first conservation efforts to protect them and their habitats. Tomas's first step in saving turtles was to teach people to see them in a different way. In Senegal and other parts of Africa, turtles were a common food source, and there was a large market for turtle meat. When Senegalese fishermen accidentally caught freshwater turtles or sea turtles in their nets (called *bycatch*), they'd eat or sell them. Because of this practice, along with the controversial bushmeat trade, thousands of turtles were being killed each year and their populations were dropping. (The bushmeat trade is the sale of wild animal meat, often to countries where the meat is considered an expensive delicacy. It's a practice that threatens wildlife populations all over the world, especially in Africa.)

Tomas taught people that turtles are vital parts of the ecosystem. For instance, tortoises and freshwater turtles are scavengers who keep the land and water clean by eating dead fish and decaying plants, and they spread seeds of trees and other plants. Sea turtles' grazing keeps seagrass beds healthy, providing habitats for other marine animals, including fish. It took a long time, but Tomas and his fellow conservationists were able to slowly change people's minds about protecting these creatures. In 2002, Tomas joined local community leaders to establish a wildlife refuge on Lac de Guiers, a lake in northern Senegal. The lake is a critical freshwater habitat for the endangered Adanson's mud turtle and the rare African manatee. "In West Africa, conservation is still a new concept. People don't know how someone can make a living by trying to save wild animals," Tomas says. "That is not something in our culture, but someone needs to make the first step, and I think that's what we're doing."

Tomas's vision for protecting turtles has grown far beyond his own country. In 2009, he founded African Chelonian Institute, the first research center on the African continent dedicated to researching and protecting all fifty-six of Africa's turtle species. The institute has a breeding facility, conducts research, and trains rangers and wildlife officials in turtle conservation. And in most places where the institute works, researchers invite the public—including schoolchildren—to watch and participate. Many African turtle and tortoise species are threatened by habitat destruction and poaching, and unlike other animal species, they aren't protected under the law. Yet despite these challenges, Tomas isn't giving up. "We still have hope. I have hope," he says. "That's why we must protect them."

THE WINTER SURVIVORS

There are places in the world where freshwater never stops flowing along riverbanks or splashing against the shore. But there are also places where—for a few months each year—water freezes as solid as stone. When this happens, some animals, such as herons and swans, leave their habitat and head to warmer destinations. But what about the ones who can't leave? How do freshwater animals **SURVIVE** when their world turns cold and food becomes scarce?

Frogs and Toads

Frogs and toads have three different hibernation strategies. Some bury themselves underground. The American toad digs a hole for itself below the *frost line*, the area where the ground won't freeze (anywhere from 6 inches to 3 feet below ground). Other species, like the northern leopard frog, spend winter underwater beneath a layer of ice. Water freezes from the top down, so even if the surface of a lake or pond is frozen, there's often plenty of water underneath. The last type of hibernation is the most amazing. Some frogs, including tree frogs, freeze solid in winter and thaw when the temperature warms again.

Beavers and Muskrats

Like amphibians, freshwater mammals have special methods for surviving cold winters. Beavers are known for the large lodges they build using mud, logs, and branches. They spend the winter in these structures, using underwater entrances to get food (branches and leaves) they've stored in the cold water below. The temperature inside a beaver lodge rarely drops below 32°F even if it's much colder outside. Muskrats, small aquatic mammals that often get mistaken for beavers, also build homes for the winter, called *push-ups*. They're smaller than beaver lodges and made from mud and cattails. Both beavers and muskrats will sometimes burrow into mud banks in colder months. They'll also sometimes become roommates—muskrats have been known to move into beaver lodges for the winter!

Fish

Freshwater fish can't migrate like birds or hibernate like mammals, so what do they do when water freezes? Most species swim to deep water and rest. Fish are *ectothermic*, or cold-blooded, so when the water temperature drops, their internal temperatures drop too. With a colder internal temperature, fish can only move very slowly and don't need to eat much, if at all. If a lake or pond is deep enough, there will always be some water below the ice where fish can wait out the winter.

BEAVE

THE BEAVER WHO BECAME WORLD-FAMOUS

The orphaned baby beaver was the size of a potato. He stared up at Nancy Coyne from inside a cardboard box. As a licensed wildlife rehabilitator, Nancy knew that unlike other animal species, the beaver would need to live in her house. In May 2020, the baby beaver moved in with Nancy's family. They named him Beave.

Beavers aren't born knowing what to eat or how to navigate river currents, swim under ice, or build dams. They learn these skills from their parents, and doing so takes at least two years. Without Beave's own family to teach him, Nancy must help him learn the skills he needs to survive in the wild. She lets him swim in her pond, gives him materials to practice building dams, and introduces him to foods like dandelion greens and cattails.

Beave has become a star on social media. But Nancy makes it clear that wild beavers are not pets. Her goal is to return Beave to nature where he belongs. When Beave turns two years old, he'll become aggressive toward his human caretakers. That's when Nancy will know that he's ready to be released into a pond and swim away into his new life.

EXPLORE A
FRESHWATER FOOD WEB

A food web, which is made of several food chains, shows what organisms eat within an ecosystem. Research and draw the food web of a freshwater habitat near you. (Visit it if you can, or use books and websites.) First, gather the following information about the habitat.

- What kind of habitat are you studying? Freshwater habitats include rivers, streams, ponds, lakes, wetlands, and estuaries.

- List all the animals and plants you see plus the animals and plants that are usually found in this type of habitat. Use a field guide or nature app (like iNaturalist) to look up species you don't know.

Next, use your observations and discoveries to draw a freshwater food web.

1. Using a field guide book or app, look up each species on your list to see what they eat (and what might eat them!). Note if the organism is a producer, consumer, or decomposer (see page 149).

2. On a piece of paper, draw and label the animals and plants in your freshwater habitat, putting them in this order: decomposers, producers, primary consumers, secondary consumers.

3. Draw arrows from each organism to the organisms that eat it. The next time you visit a freshwater habitat, think about everything that's happening right before your eyes—and beneath the surface.

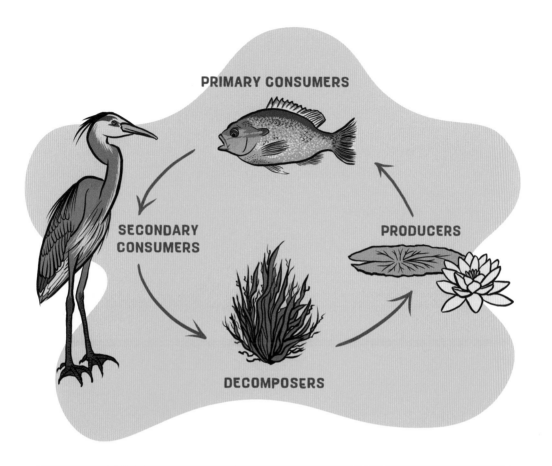

PRIMARY CONSUMERS

SECONDARY
CONSUMERS

PRODUCERS

DECOMPOSERS

PARTS OF A FOOD WEB

PRODUCERS = Organisms that make their own food, such as plants.

CONSUMERS = Organisms that eat producers (primary consumers) and organisms that eat producers and other consumers (secondary consumers).

DECOMPOSERS = These organisms (like fungi and bacteria) break down decaying animal and plant material and turn it into nutrient-rich soil.

THE ELWHA RIVER'S
SALMON AND TROUT

In rivers along North America's Pacific Coast, tiny fish hatch in the churning water and eventually follow the current to the ocean. All five species of **PACIFIC SALMON** and several **TROUT** species are born in freshwater and then live most of their lives in the open sea. When it's time to spawn and lay eggs of their own, the fish return to their home rivers in a mad rush called a *run*. They swim against the current and leap over waterfalls. It can be a long, perilous journey. But what happens when humans block their way?

Beginning in the early twentieth century, people built dams on rivers along the Pacific Coast and all over the world. One of these waterways was the Elwha River in Washington State. The Elwha River begins as a small stream dripping from a snow field in the Olympic Mountains. Then it twists and turns for forty-five miles before spilling into the sea. For most of its history, this river was home to thousands of fish. The fish were key pieces of a complex ecosystem.

In 1913, a power company built a dam on the Elwha River. A second dam was built in 1927. The dams provided electricity for the logging industry and nearby communities. But the river ecosystem—and the Lower Elwha Klallam people who lived there—paid the price. When the dams were built, two lakes flooded the valleys behind them, destroying the cultural sites and homeland of the Lower Elwha Klallam. And the dams blocked the salmon, an animal that was incredibly important to their culture and livelihood, from making their run back to their home rivers.

For the next eighty years, no wild salmon or trout could swim farther than 5 miles upriver to spawn. The salmon population plummeted from 400,000 to 3,000. Dams also prevent sediment—silt, sand, and gravel that creates riverbanks, beaches, wetlands, and estuaries—from flowing downriver. If sediment is trapped by a dam, these habitats can't exist.

In the 1980s, the Lower Elwha Klallam and conservation groups campaigned for the removal of the Elwha River dams. In 1992, Congress passed a bill that started the process, but it took another twenty years before the dams were finally dismantled. In 2014, the Elwha River flowed freely for the first time in one hundred years. At first, the water was murky with sediment—more than 30 million tons had been trapped behind the dam. But now, nearly a decade later, the river ecosystem has rebounded faster than anyone predicted.

The sediment has rebuilt riverbanks and created seventy acres of beaches and estuaries for Dungeness crabs, clams, and other animals. New forests grow in the former lakebeds, welcoming back mammals and birds. And endangered fish species like Chinook salmon and steelhead trout have returned all along the river. The increasing fish population has also attracted more seabirds and orcas to the river delta. The river's restoration isn't complete, but—like the determined salmon that swim in its waters—it's well on its way.

DRAW
FRESHWATER CREATURES

Artists have always been inspired by wildlife—and many have used their art to help animals and their habitats. Think of Beatrix Potter (see page 88) and the way she used the earnings from her book sales to conserve the countryside. Whether you draw for fun or dream of being an illustrator, drawing can be a way to learn more about wildlife. Follow the instructions below to draw freshwater animals. Then think about how you could use *your* art to help animals and animal habitats.

Pick a freshwater habitat to draw:

- pond
- lake
- stream
- river
- wetland

Based on the habitat you choose, here are some animals and plants to draw:

- **PLANTS:** cattails, reeds, grasses, lily pads, algae, moss, willows, cypress trees, palms, cottonwoods

- **ANIMALS:** ducks, geese, herons, water bugs, dragonflies, fish, beavers, muskrats, snakes, alligators, frogs, toads

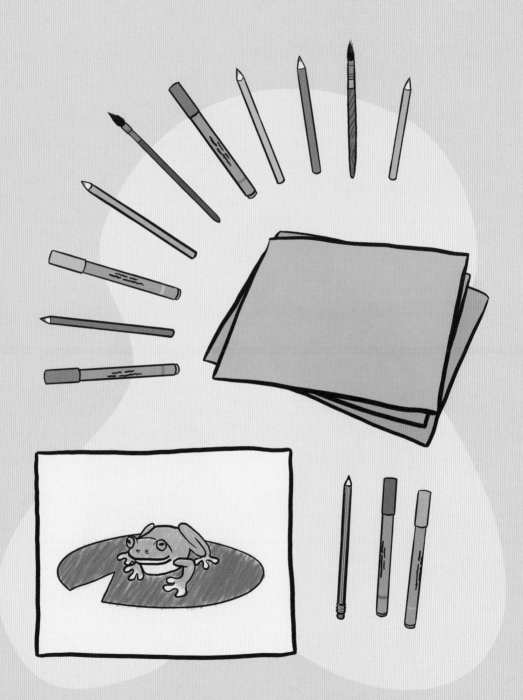

THE WATER PROTECTOR
AUTUMN PELTIER

BORN SEPTEMBER 27, 2004

"We need to protect the water today, because the longer we wait,
the sicker the plants and animals get."

—Autumn Peltier

Autumn Peltier was just twelve years old when she had the chance to meet Canada's prime minister. As she walked onstage, hundreds of people—mostly adults—were watching. It was the annual meeting of the Assembly of First Nations, a political organization of First Nations people in Canada. Autumn is Anishinaabe, one of the Indigenous Peoples of Canada. An Anishinaabe Elder had asked Autumn to attend the assembly and present the Canadian prime minister with a gift: a water bundle that included a copper bowl, tobacco, red cloth, and a cup.

Autumn's mother had spent hours making the Anishinaabe water dress she wore that day, and Autumn had spent hours thinking about what she should say. The prime minister and the Canadian government had approved the construction of oil pipelines on Indigenous lands. Autumn is a water protector, an activist who's guided by Indigenous cultural values to protect freshwater from pollution and misuse. Autumn was concerned that the new pipelines threatened Indigenous communities, especially their drinking water, surface water, and the surrounding environment. She and other concerned people had seen the environmental damage caused by burst pipelines in the United States, and they didn't want the same thing to happen in Canada.

Cameras flashed and each step Autumn took was recorded by someone's phone or camera. She knew she was supposed to smile and simply hand the prime minister the gift, but she had something to say, and it rose up like a freshwater spring. How many people—especially kids—get the chance to meet a world leader face-to-face? Autumn handed the gift to the prime minister. Then she said, "I'm very unhappy with the choices you've made." Her bold words made headlines.

Water Is Life

Autumn is from Wiikwemkoong Unceded Territory on Manitoulin Island in Lake Huron. Manitoulin is the largest freshwater island in the largest freshwater ecosystem on earth. (Not only is the island surrounded by a lake, but there are more than one hundred lakes *within* the island.) Growing up in this environment, freshwater was a special part of Autumn's life. "In my culture, my people believe that water is one of the most sacred elements," Autumn says. "It's something we honor."

From a young age, Autumn knew that freshwater was important not only to plants and wildlife but also to people. "When we're born as Anishinaabe people, we're automatically given that role to protect the water and the land," Autumn says. She lived in a place where the lakes were still clean enough to drink from and the habitat was healthy. But she soon learned that not all of Canada's water was clean or safe to drink. When she was eight years old, Autumn's family visited Serpent River First Nation for a water ceremony, and she was puzzled by what she saw. All the faucets had signs warning people not to drink or even touch the water unless they boiled it first. Autumn's mother explained that the water in that community was contaminated.

Autumn learned that many Indigenous communities in Canada—more than one hundred—did not have clean water. Sometimes water gets contaminated by outdated or broken pipes. Sometimes there isn't a water treatment plant to purify it. And sometimes a community's groundwater or surface water—such as lakes and rivers—becomes polluted. In addition to ongoing water problems that Indigenous communities were facing, Autumn learned that the Canadian government had approved the construction of another oil pipeline. The pipeline would further endanger the water in Indigenous communities. And that's what led to her brave words for the Canadian prime minister.

Protecting the Water

Autumn was not the first water protector in her family. She was taught by her great-aunt, Josephine Mandamin, an Anishinaabe Elder and the chief water commissioner for the Anishinabek Nation, a political organization that represents thirty-nine First Nations in Ontario, Canada. Josephine received national attention in the early 2000s for her "water walks" around the Great Lakes. On the walks, Josephine prayed for the health of the water and raised awareness about water pollution that was hurting the Great Lakes. In all, she walked 25,000 miles.

Josephine died in 2019 when Autumn was fifteen years old. "Her last words to me were to not stop loving the water and to keep doing the work," Autumn says. And the teenager has done just that. Following her great-aunt's death, Autumn was chosen to be the chief water commissioner for the Anishinabek Nation. As chief water commissioner, Autumn gives advice about water management to the Anishinabek Nation's leaders and citizens and helps raise awareness for all local water issues. In recent years, she's spoken at the United Nations Climate Action Summit twice and been nominated three times for the Children's International Peace Prize. Despite the global attention, Autumn stays focused on her mission. "It's not for all these awards or for the fame, it's for the water and it's for Mother Earth," Autumn says, "and the work that I'm doing is going to make an impact one day, a good impact."

STEWARDSHIP

WAYS TO CARE

YOU: Conserve Water

When people use too much water, freshwater habitats can disappear. In the western U.S., so much of the Colorado River is diverted for human use that it no longer reaches the ocean. And in central Asia, a lake that was once the fourth largest in the world—the Aral Sea—has almost completely dried up because too much of its water was drained for irrigation. Governments have a lot of power to prevent environmental disasters like these, but our individual actions matter too. Visit watercalculator.org to calculate your family's water use and learn how you can conserve water. Here are some ways to start:

Use the dishwasher. Dishwashers use less water than handwashing dishes. Scrape plates instead of pre-rinsing to save even more water.

Reuse bath towels and re-wear clothes before washing. Use the same bath towel for at least a week before washing it, and don't wash clothes unless they're dirty.

Use a rain barrel. Rain barrels collect rain that you can use to water gardens instead of turning on the hose. Ask a parent if you can set one up together.

Eat water-friendly foods. It takes a lot of water to produce and manufacture food—especially things like meat and processed products like packaged snack foods and soda. You can help conserve water by eating foods that require less water to produce, such as fresh fruits and vegetables and pasture-raised meat.

LOCAL: Adopt a Freshwater Habitat

One of the best ways to help freshwater animals is to care for their habitats. See if your community has a program that allows you to "adopt" a park that includes a freshwater habitat. This means that you (along with some friends!) spend a few hours each month cleaning up the park. It'll help your community and the wildlife that lives there.

GLOBAL: Join a Citizen Science Project

You can help scientists worldwide by joining citizen science projects that study freshwater wildlife and habitats. See if a university, environmental nonprofit, or nature center near you have citizen science opportunities for kids. Or check out these national citizen science projects in the U.S.:

FrogWatch USA: aza.org/frogwatch

EarthEcho Water Challenge: monitorwater.org

CHAPTER 7
CITY WILDLIFE

It's nighttime in London and a fox darts into a back garden. On a sunny afternoon in New Delhi, monkeys snatch food from market stands. Coyotes trot through the Denver suburbs at twilight. And along Chicago streets, pigeons patrol the sidewalks and nest on window ledges. They're not always easy to see, but animals live in cities around the world: mammals, birds, reptiles, amphibians, insects. Creatures that fly and swim and climb and scurry. Some animal species are finding ways to coexist with humans in our cities. Is it possible for *us* to coexist with them? And if so, what can we learn from our wildlife neighbors?

☙ CITY WILDLIFE FACTS ☙

1. Ants, spiders, and other insects clean up city streets by eating food waste that humans leave behind. A study in New York City showed that—on a single busy street—insects can eat **MORE THAN 2,000 POUNDS** of food waste each year.

2. Animals like coyotes, pigeons, raccoons, and opossums can thrive in cities because they're what biologists call **GENERALISTS**. This means they are able to adapt to different habitats and have a varied diet, meaning they'll eat just about anything.

3. Some animals, like monkeys, move to cities because of **HABITAT DESTRUCTION**—they have nowhere else to live. Other animals, like raccoons, make their homes in cities because urban areas have more food sources or fewer predators than their wild habitats.

4. Urban wildlife is often **NOCTURNAL** because these creatures spend the daylight hours avoiding humans, pets, and cars.

THE URBAN ECOLOGIST
DEJA PERKINS

BORN NOVEMBER 27, 1995

"Pay attention to the wildlife around you and remember that other living things share the same spaces you love. Whether it's the beach, the park, or your backyard, explore the living things that exist there."

—Deja Perkins

A little girl named Deja sat on the edge of her seat. She had seen the aquarium's dolphin show so many times that she could practically recite the trainer's lines. She knew exactly what would happen next. Yet she still grinned excitedly as the playful dolphins burst out of the water on cue, splashing the crowd and spinning in the air like gymnasts. It was amazing to see such fascinating animals right in the middle of Chicago, where buildings outnumbered trees and the most common creatures were chattering sparrows.

When Deja Perkins was growing up in the early 2000s, she thought that wildlife lived in aquariums, zoos, or distant destinations like the Caribbean Sea, where she went snorkeling. The city park in her Chicago neighborhood didn't have much wild nature but it did have tennis courts, a playground, and a wide grassy field. Deja spent a lot of time at the park—playing tennis and running around with friends—but she didn't often think about the plants and the animals that lived there. There didn't seem to be very many.

Canada geese were some of the only wildlife that seemed to live in Deja's city. When her family drove along the Lake Michigan waterfront, she'd spot flocks of the long-necked birds wandering along the road and picking at insects in the grass. To Deja, the geese along the lake and the dolphins in the aquarium were like visitors from another world—a wilder one. She wanted to explore this wilder world and the intriguing habitats where animals lived. Little did she know that one of those amazing habitats was right under her feet.

Unexpected Wildlife

Deja was a teenager when she realized something that would change her life: wildlife was all around, even in the city. She joined a youth program where she learned about the native plants and animals in the Chicago area, worked alongside other teens in the outdoors, and learned about conservation from scientists and naturalists. A year later, Deja became a leader in the program and started sharing her newfound knowledge about urban nature with others.

Because of her love of animals and science, Deja went to Tuskegee University, in Alabama, to become a veterinarian. But then she had an experience that changed her mind. One spring during college, she worked at an urban wildlife refuge in Minnesota. It was the first urban wildlife refuge she'd ever visited. Despite the surrounding city and the constant planes roaring overhead, the refuge was a hot spot for migrating birds. Deja couldn't believe all the bird species she saw that spring. "It was like I was awakened to a whole new world," she says. After that, Deja began to notice birds—and other wildlife—everywhere she went. She took up bird-watching, joined the Audubon Society, and also changed her mind about becoming a veterinarian. She wanted to study natural resources—and help connect people to nature.

A City Scientist

Deja went on to earn a graduate degree in wildlife conservation biology and became an urban ecologist, a scientist who studies the organisms that live in city environments. But her scientific work isn't only about things like birds, plants, and parks. She also studies communities and environmental justice, trying to find ways that humans and wildlife can coexist in urban places and exploring why some people, especially in cities, don't have access to nature where they live. From her research and her childhood experiences in Chicago, Deja has seen that people who live in affluent suburban neighborhoods often have nature reserves with natural green spaces and wildlife, whereas lower-income neighborhoods have parks that are designed only for sports, not wildlife. Deja hopes to be a part of changing that. "Making sure there are parks that have investment in spaces for wildlife is very important," she says.

Deja also wants to see more people of color in STEM careers and in the outdoors. As a Black woman, she sometimes feels out of place or unwelcome in these spaces. In 2020, after a Black man named Christian Cooper was falsely accused of a crime while bird-watching in New York City's Central Park, Deja and a group of her fellow naturalists decided to speak up in a new way. They launched a social media event called Black Birders Week to celebrate Black birders, scientists, and naturalists and to raise awareness about the racism and other barriers they face. Black Birders Week was so successful they plan to make it an annual event. For Deja, it's an important part of her mission to connect people to wildlife and the outdoors, no matter who they are or where they live. She says: "I believe that by exposing people, especially Black youth and young adults, to the natural sciences and the wonders of the outdoors, it will encourage them to pursue natural science careers, enjoy outdoor activities, and become stewards of the environment."

THE GOOD OF
URBAN ANIMALS

Animals who live in cities tend to have bad reputations. Squirrels, pigeons, coyotes, deer, opossums, and foxes have all been considered pests at one time or another. While there can be downsides to having wild animals in cities and neighborhoods, there are **BENEFITS** too. One good thing that all urban wildlife provides is a connection to the natural world in places where nature can be hard to find. Maybe it's time to reconsider how we look at our wildlife neighbors.

Gray Squirrels

Gray squirrels seem to be everywhere in the U.S., but they didn't choose to live in cities. In the 1880s, U.S. city governments released gray squirrels in public parks hoping their presence would make urban green spaces feel more like the countryside. They thought the animals were fun to watch and would help people reconnect to nature. And now? City squirrels are here to stay. Squirrels play an important ecological role whether they live in the city or the country. They're sometimes called "nature's gardeners" because they plant seeds and expand forests, though not on purpose. Squirrels bury a lot of seeds and nuts in the ground in *food caches*, hiding places they revisit later when they're hungry. But when squirrels forget where they buried the seeds and nuts, trees grow!

Opossums

They may look similar to rats, but opossums aren't rodents. The opossum is North America's only marsupial, a cousin of the koala and kangaroo. (And although they are sometimes called *possums*, possums are a different animal, a tree-dwelling marsupial that lives in Australia.) Like many urban animals, opossums are wrongfully accused of being aggressive and carrying diseases, but these harmless creatures have ecological benefits. Since opossums are omnivores and scavengers, they clean up dead animals (called *carrion*) from the environment. They also help humans by eating a *lot* of ticks, an insect that can carry an illness called Lyme disease. And contrary to popular belief, opossums don't carry rabies. Their low body temperature prevents them from getting the disease.

Pigeons

The urban pigeon is the distant descendant of the rock dove, a wild bird that first lived in the Mediterranean region. That's why pigeons prefer to live near tall buildings and bridges: their ancestors made their nests in rocky cliffs, not trees. These days they may seem like pests, but in some cities pigeons might be the only animals that people ever see, their one connection to a wilder world. And pigeons have a long history with humans, both as a food source and as pets. Because of their homing instinct, thousands of domesticated pigeons were used by the U.S. military as "secret agents" in World Wars I and II, delivering top-secret messages. Some of these pigeons—like Cher Ami on the following page—even received medals for their bravery!

CHER AMI

THE PIGEON WHO SAVED SOLDIERS

n World War I, more than 100,000 pigeons delivered life-saving messages. One of the most famous was a spirited female homing pigeon named Cher Ami. Homing pigeons can find their way home over long distances—up to 1,000 miles. Scientists are still trying to solve the mystery of how they do this, and they have a few theories: pigeons might use their sense of smell, follow the earth's magnetic fields, or even be able to detect special sound waves called *infrasound*.

In 1918, Cher Ami was sent to the front lines in France with the U.S. Army. She delivered a dozen top-secret messages, but her most heroic mission was her last. In October 1918, Cher Ami accompanied an American battalion into battle. The soldiers became trapped in German territory without food or water, and their own military began to fire at them by mistake.

Major Charles White Whittlesey needed to let division headquarters know the battalion's location. An urgent message was placed inside a canister on Cher Ami's leg, and the bird was released into the air. As she flew, Cher Ami was injured three times and shot down once, but she couldn't be stopped. The brave bird flew 25 miles in 25 minutes and delivered the message to headquarters. She helped save 194 lives that day. Cher Ami was celebrated as a hero and was awarded the Croix de Guerre, a French military medal given for acts of courage. A century later, she was one of the first animals to receive a new honor from the United States: the Animals in War and Peace Medal of Bravery.

DO A CITY WILDLIFE SURVEY

Animals are everywhere, even in suburbs and cities—but they're not always easy to see. To protect animals in urban environments and elsewhere, conservationists first learn about them by conducting wildlife surveys. Over time, they observe animals in the wild and collect basic information, including their behaviors and the size of their populations. In the past, some animal species have gone extinct simply because people didn't notice their dwindling numbers until it was too late! Today's wildlife biologists keep a close watch on many animal species, and they depend on volunteer citizen scientists to help gather important data. After all, the world is a big place and watching animals in the wild takes time and patience.

There may be a wildlife survey near you that's looking for volunteers. Universities, nature centers, and state-government agencies that manage natural resources are good places to look for these opportunities. But you can also do a wildlife survey of your own. Think of it as an animal scavenger hunt.

Research which animal species live in your region or state. Make a list and include mammals, birds, insects, reptiles, amphibians, and aquatic animals.

Learn which animal species have been spotted in your city or neighborhood and add these to your list. Use online sources, and also ask your family and neighbors about the animals they've seen.

Look up photos of each animal on your list so you'll learn how to recognize them. You may also want to look up their calls or songs. It's often easier to hear an animal than to spot its exact location.

Display your list in a convenient place such as a bulletin board where you can easily add to it.

Whenever you're outdoors, keep your eyes open for wildlife. When you see or hear an animal, add a tally mark next to its name on your list. You may want to keep a separate list of animal signs you spot, like tracks, nests, or burrows. Record your observations for at least two seasons and see what you discover!

WILDLIFE REHABILITATORS

Cities can be places where some animals thrive, but they can also be full of danger. Animals are regularly hurt by cars, boats, planes, and human activities. They can also be harmed by trash like plastic bags or wires. And sometimes accidents happen that don't involve people at all. Baby animals can get separated from their parents, or adult animals might wander into places where they shouldn't be. Fortunately, there are people who are trained to help animals in these situations.

WILDLIFE REHABILITATION CENTERS exist all over the world—in rural areas, suburbs, and big cities. Sometimes wildlife rehabilitation centers are part of a local Humane Society and sometimes they're an independent organization. Rehabilitators are trained and licensed to handle wild animals. Their goal isn't to keep wild animals as pets but to provide them with what they need (such as medical care or good nutrition) so they can be released back to their habitat. They sometimes need volunteers to help with their work or donate supplies. If you're not old enough to volunteer, there still could be ways to support wildlife rehabilitators in your community. (See page 108 for one idea!)

How You Can Help City Wildlife

What do you do if you see an animal that's hurt or in trouble where you live? First, don't touch the animal. You might injure it, or it could injure you. Then, tell an adult. If the animal is clearly hurt or sick, together you can contact your local Humane Society or wildlife rehabilitator for guidance. What if you find a baby animal and there isn't a parent nearby? Before rushing to help, it's important to know a few things about some animal species:

Songbirds: It's normal for baby birds to be without their parents. They can often be seen on the ground alone after leaving their nests. If the baby bird has feathers, it's called a *fledgling* and is learning to fly. The parent will still visit to feed it from time to time. No need for rescue!

Owls: Owls have a reputation for making nests that aren't very sturdy. It's common for baby owls to fall out of nests once they reach a certain age. If they're fledglings, the owl babies will be okay on the ground. If they're very young, or in trouble, you may want to contact a wildlife rehabilitator.

Rabbits: Rabbits are another species that are often alone as babies. The mother rabbit will leave her babies alone most of the time so she won't attract predators to the nest. She returns only once or twice a day to feed the baby rabbits.

Deer: Like rabbits, deer leave their young, known as *fawns*, alone for long periods to keep them safe from predators. If you find a fawn hiding in the grass, it's best to leave it alone.

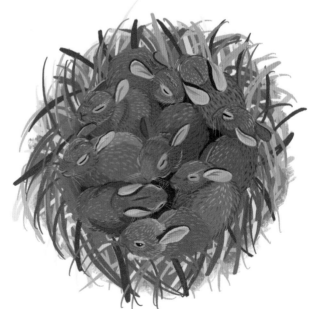

BUILD A BIRDHOUSE

Songbirds build their nests in trees, among tall grasses, tucked into rocky cliffs, or even on the ground. In cities, they often make nests on human-made structures like homes, buildings, and bridges. Unfortunately, this means that nests can end up in unsafe or inconvenient locations, like inside plant pots or above busy building entrances. To give your neighborhood birds a good place to nest, build a birdhouse (also called a nesting box). Because you'll need to use tools, this is a good project to do with an adult.

Different birds live in different types of houses. Cornell University's NestWatch website can help you figure out the type of birdhouse to build based on your local habitat and bird species and provides free instructions. (No matter which type of birdhouse you build, don't add a perch to it. Birds don't need them, and perches help predators get inside.) NestWatch also has tips for adding a nest cam so you can get a look at your bird residents! Visit nestwatch.org for more information.

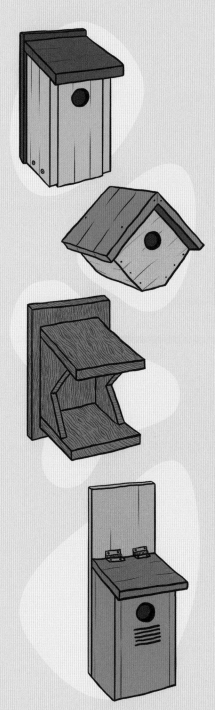

Common Birdhouses

Bluebird or Sparrow

Bluebirds nest in tree cavities but they're not always available. A small birdhouse with a roof and a 1½-inch opening is a good substitute. Because they're a similar size, sparrows will nest in this type of nesting box too.

Wren or Chickadee

Wrens and chickadees are both small birds who will make their home in a birdhouse with a 1⅛-inch opening.

Robin or Mourning Dove

Birds like robins and mourning doves don't use birdhouses, but they will build their nests on platforms. NestWatch has instructions for how to build a nest-friendly platform for these birds.

Owl

Owls are intelligent birds but they're not very good at making their own nests. (They'll often keep reusing an old nest until it falls apart!) Some species like screech owls will nest in wooden boxes.

THE FOX GUARDIAN
DORA NIGHTINGALE

BORN JANUARY 31, 1964

"I think it's so important that we look after our wildlife because it's part of the fabric of life. To have a world without birdsong or foxes or hares or badgers, it would be horrific because they're beautiful animals and there's room for all of them."

—Dora Nightingale

ong ago in the British Isles, wolves roamed the woodlands and coun-tryside. But over centuries, these wolves were relentlessly hunted and trapped, and by 1680, they were gone. Whenever an animal species disappears from an ecosystem, the habitat shifts and changes. And once the wolf was gone, a different canine took its place in the food chain: the red fox. Today there are an estimated 357,000 red foxes throughout the United Kingdom. But they don't live only in the countryside where the wolves once roamed. Foxes have found another home where they can thrive: cities.

Unexpected Visitors

Red foxes live in cities throughout the world, but nowhere are they more numer-ous than in British cities and towns. Like many city dwellers, filmmaker Dora Nightingale lived alongside foxes for years without giving them a thought. But on a summer day in 2016, Dora unexpectedly met a fox face-to-face in her back garden in West Sussex. She was watering her lawn when a young—and very curious—fox came out of the bushes. The fox started to fearlessly play in the water that Dora was spraying. "It was quite breathtaking," Dora says, "because I'd only ever seen foxes quite far away in a nature reserve through binoculars."

The fox later returned and brought three siblings with him. Like most young animals, the foxes were curious and playful. They wrestled with one another in the grass and chewed whatever they could find, including Dora's gardening gloves. They even used her lounge chair as a trampoline. Two of the foxes even-tually left, but the first fox (whom Dora named Freya before she realized he was a male) and his sister (called Faith) returned to Dora's garden every day.

Filming Foxes

As a child in Bavaria, Germany, Dora had always felt a connection to animals. She and her family often helped injured animals like hedgehogs and birds.

(Once, a pair of hedgehogs they rescued spent the winter hibernating in their cellar!) And when Dora got her first camera at age six, she immediately turned her lens on nature. By the time she was a teenager, Dora was spending hours taking animal photos and developing them in her father's darkroom, a special room where film photos are processed.

The day Dora met a fox in her garden, it was only natural that she'd pick up her camera and start filming. By that time she had studied film at the University of Cologne and was working as a filmmaker. But foxes were new to her. "I knew nothing about foxes at the time, and their beauty, intelligence, boundless energy, and happy playfulness captured my heart," Dora says. Dora filmed nearly 700 hours of footage of Freya and Faith's visits, and she used the footage to make a documentary. In 2017 the film, *Foxed*, won an award at a wildlife film festival, and it has been seen by thousands of people. It was the beginning of Dora's mission to tell truthful and positive stories about foxes.

In many cultures and places, foxes have long been seen as sneaky tricksters who cause trouble, not the kind of creatures people want in their neighborhood. In fairy tales and fables, they've been unfairly described as deceitful or even villainous. This negative reputation persists today, and many people think that foxes are destructive or dangerous pests. But Dora says that this bad reputation isn't based on reality. "Foxes are not evil or sly, nor are they vermin," Dora says. "Foxes are highly intelligent, iconic, and indigenous animals that just want to live in peace, and they do play a very important role in the ecosystem."

Foxes have been able to survive in unusual circumstances because they're smart and adaptable. Like many city-dwelling animals, they have a varied diet that includes earthworms, beetles, small rodents, fruits and vegetables, birds, and even roadkill and trash. (And contrary to popular opinion, foxes are not usually a threat to humans or cats. Both people and cats are much more likely to be injured by domestic dogs than foxes.)

Since that summer day when she met Freya, Dora has been using her skills as a filmmaker to help change people's minds and show them what foxes are really like. She founded Fox Guardians, a nonprofit organization that produces educational films about foxes and works to protect them in both rural and urban environments. Using social media, Dora shares stories, photos, and videos and encourages others to take action on behalf of foxes and become "fox guardians" too. She also has helped rehabilitate foxes, worked with city governments to stop the destruction of fox dens, and campaigned against fox hunting in the U.K. "Now my life is all about foxes," Dora says. "I film foxes, write and post about foxes, campaign and march for foxes, strive to be a voice for foxes."

STEWARDSHIP

WAYS TO CARE

YOU: Keep Trash Away from Animals

There's one thing that can easily turn a city-dwelling animal into a nuisance: trash. Animals are on a constant search for their next meal, and the trash that humans leave behind can seem like a buffet to a hungry creature. A food source like trash also encourages animals to return to places that are unsafe for them, like busy streets and parking lots. If your family leaves trash containers outdoors, make sure they're tightly closed and secure, especially at night. If you live in a city that has bears or larger mammals, you'll need a trash container that's specially designed to keep them out.

LOCAL: Support Wildlife Corridors

A public park or undeveloped lot can be an oasis for urban wildlife. But for animals to thrive, they need safe ways to travel from one natural habitat to another. City planners can create *wildlife corridors* between green spaces by planting trees or setting aside parcels of undeveloped land. This helps animals move freely while avoiding roads and commercial development. Natural features like rivers can also act as wildlife corridors. Does your city have wildlife corridors? Look at a map to see how parks or green spaces are connected. If they aren't, is there a way to connect them by planting trees or vegetation? Consider writing to your local parks department to share your ideas.

GLOBAL: Protect Habitats Beyond the City

Not all animals can survive in cities. And not all animals can (or should) coexist with humans in urban environments. All over the world, animals need their habitats protected so they don't have to live among humans. Wildlife such as bears, mountain lions, tigers, and monkeys often show up in cities, but they're better off in the wild. Here are some organizations that protect wildlife habitat and let kids and teens get involved in their work:

Roots and Shoots: rootsandshoots.org

Wildlife Warriors: wildlifewarriors.org

Earth Rangers: earthrangers.com

INTO THE WILD WORLD

Reading this book is just one step in learning about our world's wildlife and the part we can play in helping all earth's creatures thrive. There's so much more to discover and do! If you've been inspired by the stories in this book and want to learn more (or take action), revisit the Field Trip and Stewardship sections of each chapter. And check out some of the organizations below.

Insects

PLANET BEE FOUNDATION planetbee.org

MONARCH WATCH monarchwatch.org

NATIONAL WILDLIFE FOUNDATION'S NATIVE PLANT FINDER nwf.org/nativeplantfinder

Birds

NATIONAL AUDUBON SOCIETY audubon.org

AUDUBON BIRD GUIDE audubon.org/app

MERLIN BIRD ID merlin.allaboutbirds.org

CORNELL LAB OF ORNITHOLOGY birds.cornell.edu

PROJECT FEEDERWATCH feederwatch.org

NESTWATCH nestwatch.org

GREAT BACKYARD BIRD COUNT birdcount.org

Reptiles and Amphibians

FROGID frogid.net.au

WILDLIFE WARRIORS wildlifewarriors.org

FROGWATCH USA aza.org/frogwatch

Land Animals

MYNATURE: ANIMAL TRACKS mynatureapps.com/mynature-animal-tracks

BAT CONSERVATION INTERNATIONAL batcon.org

HUMANE SOCIETY OF THE UNITED STATES humanesociety.org

EARTH RANGERS earthrangers.com

ROOTS AND SHOOTS rootsandshoots.org

WORLD WILDLIFE FUND worldwildlife.org

Ocean Creatures

FRIENDS OF THE SEA OTTER seaotters.org

SAVE THE WHALES savethewhales.org

PROJECT AWARE projectaware.org/sharks

BILLION OYSTER PROJECT billionoysterproject.org

SEA TURTLE CONSERVANCY conserveturtles.org

WILD OCEANS wildoceans.org

Freshwater Life

WATER CALCULATOR watercalculator.org

FROGWATCH USA aza.org/frogwatch

EARTHECHO WATER CHALLENGE monitorwater.org

City Wildlife

HUMANE SOCIETY OF THE UNITED STATES humanesociety.org

NESTWATCH nestwatch.org

FOX GUARDIANS foxguardians.co.uk

ROOTS AND SHOOTS rootsandshoots.org

WILDLIFE WARRIORS wildlifewarriors.org

EARTH RANGERS earthrangers.com

SELECTED BIBLIOGRAPHY

For a complete list of references consulted, visit quirkbooks.com/TheWildWorldHandbookCreatures.

Chapter 1: Insects

Ferrari, Michelle, dir. *American Experience*, season 29, episode 4, "Rachel Carson." Aired January 24, 2017, on WGBH.

Lotzof, Kerry. "Maria Sibylla Merian: metamorphosis unmasked by art and science." National History Museum. https://www.nhm.ac.uk/discover/maria-sibylla-merian-metamorphosis-art-and-science.html.

Klein, Joanna. "A Pioneering Woman of Science Re-Emerges After 300 Years." *New York Times*, January 23, 2017. https://www.nytimes.com/2017/01/23/science/maria-sibylla-merian-metamorphosis-insectorum-surinamensium.html.

Krulwich, Robert. "Six-Legged Giant Finds Secret Hideaway, Hides for 80 Years." NPR, February 29, 2012. https://www.npr.org/sections/krulwich/2012/02/24/147367644/six-legged-giant-finds-secret-hideaway-hides-for-80-years.

Scott, Alec. "Where Do You Go, My Lovelies?" *University of Toronto* magazine, August 24, 2015. https://magazine.utoronto.ca/campus/history/where-do-you-go-my-lovelies-norah-and-fred-urquhart-monarch-butterfly-migration.

"The Story of Silent Spring." National Resources Defense Council, August 13, 2015. https://www.nrdc.org/stories/story-silent-spring.

Wulf, Andrea. "The Woman Who Made Science Beautiful." *Atlantic*, January 19, 2016. https://www.theatlantic.com/science/archive/2016/01/the-woman-who-made-science-beautiful/424620.

Chapter 2: Birds

Alex Foundation. "Alex: 1976–2007." https://alexfoundation.org/the-birds/alex.

Alvis, Alexandra K. "Elizabeth Gould: An Accomplished Woman." *Unbound* blog. Smithsonian Libraries and Archives. March 29, 2018. https://blog.library.si.edu/blog/2018/03/29/elizabeth-gould-an-accomplished-woman.

Bailey, Florence Merriam. "How to Conduct Field Classes." *Bird-Lore*, February 1900.

Chisholm, A.H. "Gould, Elizabeth (1804–1841)." Australian Dictionary of Biography, National Centre of Biography, Australian National University, https://adb.anu.edu.au/biography/gould-elizabeth-2112/text2665, published first in hardcopy 1966.

Editors of *Encyclopedia Britannica*. "Florence Augusta Merriam Bailey." *Encyclopedia Britannica*, July 20, 1998. https://www.britannica.com/biography/Florence-Augusta-Merriam-Bailey.

Serratore, Angela. "Keeping Feathers Off Hats—And On Birds." Smithsonianmag.com, May 15, 2018. https://www.smithsonianmag.com/history/migratory-bird-act-anniversary-keeping-feathers-off-hats-180969077.

"Fact Sheet: Natural History, Ecology, and Recovery." U.S. Fish & Wildlife Service. Midwest Region – Bald and Golden Eagles. Revised July 2019. https://www.fws.gov/midwest/eagle/Nhistory/biologue.html.

Wade, Lisa. "The Bird Hat Craze That Sparked a Preservation Movement." *Pacific Standard*, updated June 14, 2017. https://psmag.com/social-justice/bird-hat-craze-sparked-preservation-movement-92745.

Wolfe, Jonathan. "Overlooked No More: Florence Merriam Bailey, Who Defined Modern Bird-Watching." *New York Times*, July 17, 2019.

Chapter 3: Reptiles and Amphibians

"American Alligator." U.S. Fish & Wildlife Service. February 2008. https://www.fws.gov/uploadedFiles/American-Alligator-Fact-Sheet.pdf.

Boulenger, E. G. "Dr. Joan B. Procter." *Nature*, no. 128 (October 17, 1931): 664–5. https://doi.org/10.1038/128664b0.

Dowling, H. G., and George R. Zug. "Reptile." *Encyclopedia Britannica*, updated February 11, 2021. https://www.britannica.com/animal/reptile.

Duellman, W. E., and George R. Zug. "Amphibian." *Encyclopedia Britannica*, updated February 4, 2020. https://www.britannica.com/animal/amphibian.

Galapagos Conservancy. "Lonesome George." https://www.galapagos.org/about_galapagos/about-galapagos/biodiversity/lonesome-george.

Pettit, Rebekah. "Reptile Conservation Success Story: The American Alligator." *Reptiles*, October 1, 2018. https://www.reptilesmagazine.com/reptile-conservation-success-story-the-american-alligator.

Procter, Joan B. "Dragons That Are Alive To-Day." In *Wonders of Animal Life: An Illustrated Encyclopaedia by Famous Writers on Natural History*, edited by J. A. Hammerton. London: The Waverley Book Company Ltd., 1920.

"Reptile House." ZLS London Zoo. https://www.zsl.org/zsl-london-zoo/exhibits/reptile-house.

"Steve Irwin." Australia Zoo. https://www.australiazoo.com.au/about-us/the-irwins/steve.

Chapter 4: Land Animals

"Beatrix Potter, the Lake District and the National Trust." National Trust. https://www.nationaltrust.org.uk/beatrix-potter-gallery-and-hawkshead/features/beatrix-potter-the-lake-district-and-the-national-trust.

Burns, Ken, dir. *The National Parks: America's Best Idea*. Public Broadcasting Service, 2009.

Collins, Britt. "Christian the lion, our joy and pride." *Guardian*, May 27, 2011. https://www.theguardian.com/lifeandstyle/2011/may/28/christian-the-lion-rendall-bourke.

George Wright Society. "Who Was George Meléndez Wright?" https://www.georgewrightsociety.org/gmw.

"Gray Wolf." Smithsonian's National Zoo & Conservation Biology Institute. https://nationalzoo.si.edu/animals/gray-wolf.

Gristwood, Sarah. *The Story of Beatrix Potter.* London: Pavilion Books, 2016.

Holland, Jennifer S. "Pandas Get to Know Their Wild Side." *National Geographic*, August 2016. https://www.nationalgeographic.com/magazine/article/giant-pandas-wild-animals-national-parks.

"Meerkat." Smithsonian's National Zoo & Conservation Biology Institute. https://nationalzoo.si.edu/animals/meerkat.

National Geographic. "Raising Cute Pandas: It's Complicated." July 14, 2016. Video, 2:40. https://www.youtube.com/watch?v=v_cpPMjE0vU.

Chapter 5: Ocean Creatures

"Being the Manatees' Best Friend." *World Wildlife* magazine, Summer 2015. https://www.worldwildlife.org/magazine/issues/summer-2015/articles/being-the-manatees-best-friend.

"Dr. Eugenie Clark (1922-2015)." National Ocean Service. https://oceanservice.noaa.gov/news/may15/eugenie-clark.html.

"Explorers at Work: Jamal Galves." *National Geographic.* https://www.nationalgeographic.org/projects/explorers/jamal-galves.

Kanai, Lang. "How Did Manatees Inspire Mermaid Legends?" *National Geographic*, November 25, 2014. https://www.nationalgeographic.com/animals/article/141124-manatee-awareness-month-dugongs-animals-science.

McFadden, Robert D. "Eugenie Clark, Scholar of the Life Aquatic, Dies at 92." *New York Times*, February 25, 2015. https://www.nytimes.com/2015/02/26/us/eugenie-clark-scholar-of-the-life-aquatic-dies-at-92.html.

McLeish, Todd. *Return of the Sea Otter: The Story of the Animal That Evaded Extinction on the Pacific Coast.* Seattle: Sasquatch Books, 2018.

O'Grady, Cathleen. "The Oddball Dolphin of Dingle." *Hakai* magazine, July 14, 2020. https://www.hakaimagazine.com/features/the-oddball-dolphin-of-dingle.

O'Loughlin, Ed. "Fungie, Ireland's Missing Dolphin, 'Goes With the Tide.'" *New York Times*, October 28, 2020.

Chapter 6: Freshwater Life

Diagne, Tomas. "The African Chelonian Institute: Protecting the Turtles of Africa." *Reptiles*, January 18, 2018. https://www.reptilesmagazine.com/the-african-chelonian-institute-protecting-the-turtles-of-africa.

Leadership for Conservation in Africa. "Saving African freshwater turtles and tortoises." September 27, 2020. Video, 1:10:15. https://www.youtube.com/watch?v=Lx7Au8pAFYE&t=864s.

Nijhuis, Michelle. "World's Largest Dam Removal Unleashes U.S. River After Century of Electric Production." *National Geographic*, August 27, 2014. https://www.nationalgeographic.com/science/article/140826-elwha-river-dam-removal-salmon-science-olympic.

Raising the Wild. "Great Interview Question & Answer Session." January 1, 2021. Video, 10:39. https://www.youtube.com/watch?v=CxagJ_3FoFw.

"Tomas Diagne." African Aquatic Conservation Fund. https://africanaquaticconservation.org/team/tomas-diagne.

Tusk. "Tomas Diagne - Senegal." November 21, 2019. Video, 4:44. https://www.youtube.com/watch?v=0aq-Hcclu30.

Wight, Andrew. "How Did This Senegalese Scientist Meet Prince William? Turtles!" *Forbes*, December 11, 2019. https://www.forbes.com/sites/andrewwight/2019/12/11/how-did-this-senegalese-scientist-meet-prince-william-turtles/.

Chapter 7: City Wildlife

Barrera, Jorge. "The gift and a tearful pipeline plea: Autumn Peltier, 12, reveals what she told PM Trudeau." APTN National News, December 7, 2016. https://www.aptnnews.ca/national-news/the-gift-a-tearful-pipeline-plea-autumn-peltier-12-reveals-what-she-told-pm-trudeau.

Becking, Marci. "Autumn Peltier going to the United Nations to share her message about water." *Anishinabek News*, September 23, 2019. https://anishinabeknews.ca/2019/09/23/autumn-peltier-going-to-the-united-nations-to-share-her-message-about-water.

Chicago Audubon Society. "Finding My Flock: A Conservation Story." August 18, 2020. Video, 55:04. https://www.youtube.com/watch?v=BzoiDNJhm24.

Dell'Amore, Christine. "How Wild Animals Are Hacking Life in the City." *National Geographic*, April 18, 2016. https://www.nationalgeographic.com/animals/article/160418-animals-urban-cities-wildlife-science-coyotes.

Kelly, John. "America's city squirrels have humans to thank for giving them a home." *Washington Post*, April 5, 2014. https://www.washingtonpost.com/local/americas-city-squirrels-have-humans-to-thank-for-giving-them-a-home/2014/04/05/e0786c20-ba8e-11e3-9a05-c739f29ccb08_story.html.

Nature on PBS. "Mythbusting Opossum Facts." August 10, 2020. Video, 3:16. https://www.youtube.com/watch?v=fLYofE1WFMs.

Nightingale, Dora, dir. *Foxed*. Fox Guardians, 2017. https://www.youtube.com/watch?v=i4HHHVK-mCDs&t=5s.

TIFF Originals. "Autumn Peltier and Greta Thunberg." September 20, 2020. Video, 32:09. https://www.youtube.com/watch?v=_h1JbSBqZpQ.

INDEX